An Advertiser's Guide To Better Radio Advertising

AN ADVERTISER'S GUIDE TO BETTER RADIO ADVERTISING

Tune in to the power of the brand conversation medium

Andrew Ingram
and
Mark Barber

John Wiley & Sons, Ltd

Other Wiley Editorial Offices

John Wiley & Sons Inc., 111 River Street, Hoboken, NJ 07030, USA

Jossey-Bass, 989 Market Street, San Francisco, CA 94103-1741, USA

Wiley-VCH Verlag GmbH, Boschstr. 12, D-69469 Weinheim, Germany

John Wiley & Sons Australia Ltd, 33 Park Road, Milton, Queensland 4064, Australia

John Wiley & Sons (Asia) Pte Ltd, 2 Clementi Loop #02-01, Jin Xing Distripark, Singapore
129809

John Wiley & Sons Canada Ltd, 22 Worcester Road, Etobicoke, Ontario, Canada M9W 1L1

Wiley also publishes its books in a variety of electronic formats. Some content that appears in
print may not be available in electronic books.

British Library Cataloguing in Publication Data

A catalogue record for this book is available from the British Library

ISBN 13   978-0-470-01292-5 (HB)
ISBN 10   0-470-01292-7 (HB)

Typeset in 10.5/16 pt Trump Medieval by SNP Best-set Typesetter Ltd., Hong Kong
Printed and bound in Great Britain by TJ International Ltd, Padstow, Cornwall, UK
This book is printed on acid-free paper responsibly manufactured from sustainable forestry
in which at least two trees are planted for each one used for paper production.

Contents

Foreword

Radio is an extraordinary medium. It has a unique power to enter your consciousness quite unexpectedly with news, drama, advice, poetry, humour . . . listeners often refer to the medium as a friend that lifts their mood. It is also very significant now as a channel for advertisers, with two-thirds of the population listening to commercial radio each week.

And yet, how often do you hear radio advertisements which harness the true power of the medium? Not often enough. This must be, in part at least, because radio is so flexible as an advertising medium – you can book it late, the ads can be made quickly and at relatively low cost and this inevitably leads to average advertising, or worse.

So what can you as an advertiser do to ensure your standards of creativity are as high as possible?

I would have two recommendations. First, take radio more seriously – if you do, your teams will come with you. Second, have a look at this book – it's full of practical advice to help you manage the process, and the people involved, more effectively. And ultimately, it's this that can make all the difference.

Jo Kenrick
Director of marketing communications, Camelot

How to use this book

If you are an advertiser who is absolutely happy with the quality of their radio advertising, you probably don't need this book.

We designed it for advertisers who may be using radio at the moment but feel their on-air messages could be improved – made more memorable, more persuasive, more believable, leaving a better impression with the listener.

You can read this book as a dip-in (someone told us they'd keep it in the office toilet), or from start to finish. The first section explains what radio is like as a medium, the second looks at techniques for harnessing its power; then in section three we consider a new way of looking at radio (as "new media"). Finally in section four we offer the "Seven-Step Guide to Better Radio Advertising" – if you're going to put the bookmark anywhere, put it here.

Importantly, this is about audio, and many of the points are easy to understand once you hear the commercials we discuss. To hear them, simply go to www.better-radio-advertising.co.uk.

By the way, if you really are an advertiser who is absolutely happy with their radio advertising, we'd really like to hear from you. You must be doing something right that others can learn from.

Acknowledgements

We are grateful to the following companies for permission to reproduce material throughout this book:

AC Nielsen – Figure 4.2

Advertising Association – Figure 1.9

BARB/RAJAR Ltd – Figure 2.6

BNRC/MED Medial Lab – Figure 7.6

CRCA/OFCOM – Figure 1.13

Future Foundation – Figure 7.2

John Grant and the Radio Advertising Bureau – Figure 7.4

The Henley Centre Ltd – Figures 7.1, 7.7

Martin Sims – Figures 5.2, 5.3

Megalab – Figure 2.13

Millward Brown – Figure 4.3

Newslink – Figure 2.4

Nielsen Media Research (UK) Ltd – Figure 1.8

OFCOM – Figure 1.2

Radio Advertising Bureau – Figures 1.1, 1.7, 1.10, 1.11, 1.12, 2.1, 2.2, 2.3, 2.5, 2.8, 2.9, 2.10, 2.11, 2.12, 2.14, 2.15, 2.16, 2.17, 2.18, 3.1, 3.2, 3.3, 4.1, 4.5, 5.1, 5.4, 6.1, 6.2, 7.5, 8.1, 8.2, 8.3, 8.4, 8.5, 8.6, 8.7, 8.8, 8.9, 8.10

Radio Marketing Service GmbH – Figure 4.4

RAJAR Ltd – Figures 1.3, 1.4, 1.5, 1.6, 1.14

About the Authors

Mark Barber

After graduating from the University of Life, Mark spent 18 years as a media planner in a variety of media agencies before joining the Radio Advertising Bureau in 2001. He has been using radio as an advertising medium since 1983, during which time his perspective has moved from audience cost-per-thousands to the communication benefits of the medium.

Mark's previous contributions to radio literature include *Understanding Radio, the Brand Conversation Medium* and *Radio Advertising Effectiveness for Dummies*. In his spare time, he supports Charlton Athletic, is teaching himself to speak Turkish, and entertains his children with bad jokes and poorly executed magic tricks.

Andrew Ingram

Andrew has a broad-based experience in advertising and media. After graduating from Cambridge in 1979, he started commercial life in the advertisement department of the *Daily Mail*, going on through quantitative research, and qualitative research, and eventually moving into account planning before joining the RAB in 1992.

Andrew's previous books include *Wireless Wisdom* and *Understanding Radio*. He is a regular speaker at media and advertising conferences across the globe. In his spare time, he indulges in daughters and classic cars, and an art project involving old plastic bags in trees.

The authors work together at the Radio Advertising Bureau on a daily basis, helping advertisers and agencies overcome the barriers that are preventing them from using radio advertising more effectively. It is this experience that has informed the development of this book.

SECTION 1
THE CASE FOR CHANGE

'I think for a lot of people in advertising, commercial radio is like bus travel. We know it exists but it's not part of our lifestyle. It's a culture we don't know a lot about.'

Advertiser delegate at RAB training

In this section we review the scale of commercial radio in the UK and the benefits it offers advertisers. We consider the medium from the listener's perspective and how advertising works within this context. We then demonstrate how existing practices are limiting advertising effectiveness and why they need to change.

Chapter 1   The Scale of the Medium

- The development of commercial radio in the UK
- Measurement and growth of the commercial radio audience
- Who listens to commercial radio?
- Radio's status as an advertising medium
- What does the future hold for commercial radio?
- Summary

Chapter 2   The 'True' Radio Context

- Why and how people listen
- Radio's media attributes
- How radio communicates
- Effectiveness of the medium
- Summary

Chapter 3   The Need for a Different Approach

- Why the need for a different approach?
- Why does radio advertising have to be creative?
- Why aren't we better at using radio?
- The challenges and opportunities of the medium
- Summary

1
The Scale of the Medium

Commercial radio has had to fight hard for its place in UK media because of the historical dominance of BBC radio services, but it is now a genuine mass medium. This chapter takes a closer look at the nature of that growth.

There are more stations and more listeners – over 30 million people listen each week – and increased advertising revenue has followed them. At the same time, station segmentation means that it is possible to reach finely targeted subgroups.

This chapter also looks at the way radio listening is likely to develop in the digital age.

1.1 The development of commercial radio in the UK

Commercial radio is the youngest member of the UK's 'traditional' commercial media canon, having only started broadcasting in October 1973.

The first ILR (Independent Local Radio) station on air was LBC, followed a week later by Capital Radio, both in London. The first ILR station to start broadcasting outside London was Radio Clyde in Glasgow on New Year's Eve 1973.

Across the next two years, sixteen new stations were launched before the development of ILR was halted in 1976 by a new Labour government, cautious about commercial organisations running radio stations.

With the return of a Conservative government in 1979, the ILR network was given permission to expand again, and throughout the early 1980s many new stations were launched, gradually filling in gaps in coverage across the UK. This led to a steady growth in the number of ILR stations across the early 1980s, building loyal audiences through an eclectic programme mix.

The next step change came in 1989 with the government's desire to make better use of the radio spectrum. This led to ILR stations being required to run different services on their FM and AM transmitters, which gave rise to the 'Gold' format stations playing oldies and classic hits.

In 1990, the first *incremental* radio stations went on air. In essence, these were additional radio services introduced into areas already served by an ILR station. The new incremental stations had to offer output not already available on ILR, such as specialist music or unique programmes for a specific section of the community.

In the Broadcasting Act of 1990, the government deregulated broadcasting and created the Radio Authority to oversee further development of independent radio. The 'lighter touch' of the Radio Authority removed many of the technical, programming and local ownership requirements from ILR, and mergers and takeovers began to gather pace, leading to the development of many of today's major radio groups.

The Radio Authority introduced many new local radio licences during the 1990s, filling any remaining gaps in coverage, as well as creating new *regional* licences. However, the biggest change came with the introduction of three *national* licences, leading to the launch of Classic FM in September 1992, Virgin Radio in April 1993 and Talk Radio UK in February 1995.

By the late 1990s, the number of AM or FM frequencies remaining for further large-scale expansion of the radio market was limited. To allow for continued development to take place, a new broadcasting band and a new technology – Digital Audio Broadcasting (DAB) – was introduced.

Instead of having a different frequency for each radio station, DAB combined several services together into 'multiplexes'. Each multiplex was subdivided into further separate channels, allowing up to ten radio stations to be transmitted within the same amount of radio spectrum previously required by one single analogue FM station.

New regional and local AM and FM licences continued to be awarded (albeit at a slower pace) alongside the development of stations on the DAB platform – Digital One, the national commercial DAB multiplex, was launched in 1999, carrying the existing national analogue station brands in addition to some new digital-only station brands.

The Communications Act of 2003 saw the newly created communications regulatory body Ofcom take on responsibility for regulating radio. Ownership restrictions were liberalised further to allow a minimum of '2 + BBC' owners in any individual market, and the expected consolidation arising from this ruling has now begun with the merger of Capital Radio Group and GWR.

In many parts of the country the FM spectrum is now fully used. However, a number of frequencies and areas for new stations have been identified and these will be licensed where possible. It is estimated that approximately 30 new FM licences will be issued over the next three years.

In July 2004, Ofcom passed new legislation setting out rules for *community* radio – highly localised services (typically with a radius of 5 km) catering for a particular area or community of interest.

In the coming years, community radio is likely to significantly increase the number of independent radio stations across the UK, alongside the continued issuing of new FM licences. However, these will be run primarily for social gain in the community, not for profit, and only a limited number are likely to take advertising.

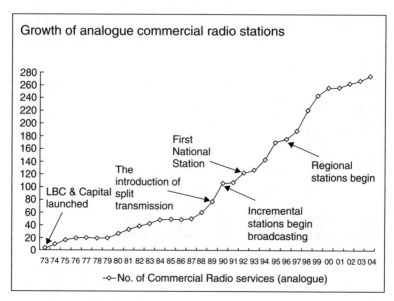

Figure 1.1 Growth of analogue commercial radio stations

In Autumn 2004, 31 years after commercial radio first launched, there were 274 analogue stations (a combination of national, regional, local, incremental and community) broadcasting in the UK (see Figure 1.1).

The UK is also the world leader in DAB digital radio, with 130 stations currently broadcasting a combination of new formats and existing analogue radio brands, bringing much greater listener choice across most parts of the country (see Figure 1.2).

1.2 Measurement and growth of the commercial radio audience

For the first few years, the size of the radio audience was gauged by individual stations' own estimates. The first ILR industry-

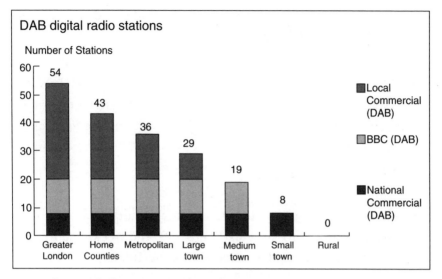

Figure 1.2 Typical availability of DAB digital radio stations by area

wide survey, JICRAR (Joint Industry Committee for Radio Audience Research) was launched in 1975. Alongside JICRAR, the BBC ran its own telephone panel survey on a day-after-recall basis, which continued up to 1992.

In 1992, responsibility for measuring both the commercial and BBC radio audience was handed to RAJAR (Radio Joint Audience Research Ltd). The RAJAR methodology was based on listeners filling in seven-day self-completion diaries.

In 1998 there was a slight methodology change to adjust the diaries to the growth in the number of stations. A 'personalised' diary, customised to include only the stations listened to by each individual respondent, replaced the previously preprinted list of stations in the diary. This methodology is still operating at the time of writing, however RAJAR is currently engaged in a rigorous process of testing the potential of different electronic systems for measuring radio listening.

So what has happened to the commercial radio audience across 30 years of measurement?

JICRAR initially revealed that 12 million adults a week were listening to the 18 ILR stations on air. These listeners were younger and reflected the demographic profile of the local area more closely than BBC listeners – a statistic that has remained consistent to the current day.

By 1980 this had grown to 14.5 million adults and with the expansion of ILR across the early eighties, the weekly commercial radio audience reached 22.5 million by 1985.

Audience growth enjoyed further boosts across the late 1980s and early 1990s through the introduction of split transmission (FM/AM) and the launch of incremental stations providing new formats (e.g. Jazz FM and Kiss) appealing to specific demographic groups/communities of interest.

Throughout the nineties, commercial radio audiences continued to grow as additional listening choices provided new listeners with reasons to tune in. This was exemplified by the launch of the first national station, Classic FM, which attracted an audience of 4.2 million adults within months of launch. Figure 1.3 demonstrates the variety and popularity of the different formats.

However, another trend was also becoming evident – not only were more people tuning in, but they were listening for longer. In 1999, when the new RAJAR methodology was introduced, approximately two-thirds of the UK population was listening to commercial radio for an average of 15 hours each week.

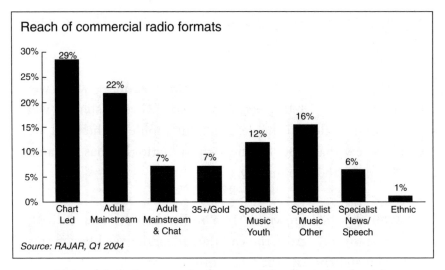

Figure 1.3 Audience reach of commercial radio stations by style

Over the last five years, total radio listening (calculated in terms of numbers of listeners and how long they listen for, and expressed as 'total hours') has increased by 7 %. Commercial radio's share of listening vs. the BBC has declined across this period, but in absolute terms it is still accounting for a growing number of listening hours (Figure 1.4).

Latest data (RAJAR Q2, 2004, available at www.rajar.co.uk) reveals that 31.4 million adults listen to commercial radio for an average of 15.4 hours every week. According to research conducted by the RAB (Figure 1.12), radio is second only to TV in terms of the amount of time people spend with the medium.

1.3 Who listens to commercial radio?

Overall, commercial radio has always attracted a younger set of listeners than the BBC. When RAJAR first posted listening figures in 1992, commercial radio was particularly strong in reaching the 15–44 age group, especially compared with the BBC.

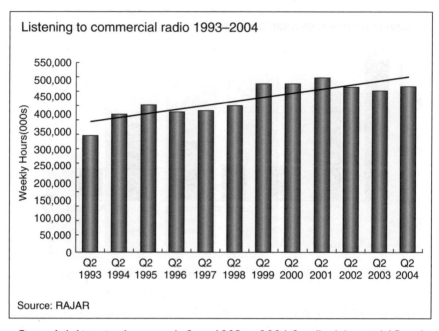

Figure 1.4 Listening hour trends from 1993 to 2004 for all adults aged 15 and over

This listener group became known as *the commercial radio generation* – people who had grown up, or were growing up, with commercial radio as their preferred choice of listening.

In 2004, this age group is still dominant in the commercial radio listening profile (see Figure 1.5) but a number of factors have helped to increase commercial listening amongst other demographics.

The first of these factors is the cohort effect – people who have grown up as commercial radio listeners remaining as such, even as they enter demographic breaks traditionally associated with listening to BBC stations.

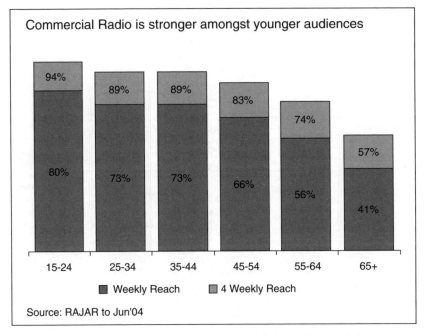

Figure 1.5 Commercial radio's weekly and four-weekly reach by age

The other important factor has been the development of a greater variety of station formats catering for a broader set of tastes. The appeal of different station formats for different audiences is highlighted in Figure 1.6.

Commercial radio is also very strong in reaching children compared with the BBC. Historically, the majority of this listening has been considered incidental, driven by their parents' choice of station. However, new station formats aimed specifically at children (e.g. Capital Disney and Abracadabra, both on DAB), combined with the increased availability of radio listening via the television, are leading to more selective and active listening amongst this audience.

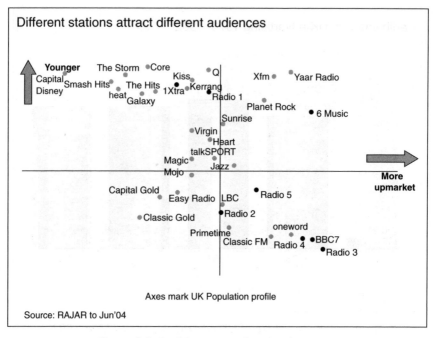

Figure 1.6 Age/class map of national stations

1.4 Radio's status as an advertising medium

In the early weeks following commercial radio's launch in October 1973, advertising revenue exceeded initial expectations, however, this was not to last, and the first ILR stations soon found themselves struggling to win significant revenue from other media.

It wasn't until the establishment of the audience measurement system JICRAR, which provided essential information about how many were listening to which stations and when, that advertisers began to take to the medium. Radio revenue was further boosted by the ITV technicians' strike of 1979.

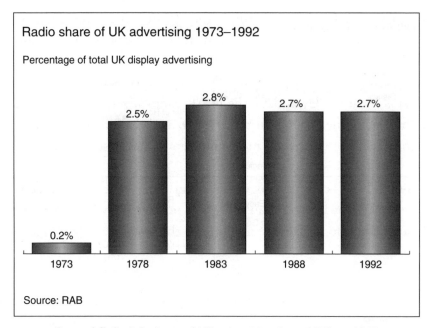

Figure 1.7 Radio's share of UK advertising from 1973 to 1992

However, despite continued and significant audience growth, radio's overall share of advertising revenue resolutely remained between 2.5 % and 2.8 % throughout the late 1970s, the whole of the 1980s and into the early 1990s (see Figure 1.7) – hence radio's old nickname of the '2 % medium'.

1992 was a pivotal year for commercial radio. The launch that year of a new audience research system (RAJAR), the launch of the first national station (Classic FM) and the launch of a unified business-to-business marketing strategy (Radio Advertising Bureau) contributed to a quantum leap in the industry's fortunes.

As a result, many national advertisers began to reappraise the medium and growth from this sector helped advertising revenue to rise sharply across the first half of the 1990s. Continued evolution of the medium in terms of station and audience growth, coupled with the RAB's marketing effort, mean that radio is playing an increasingly prominent role amongst blue chip advertisers.

Looking at the latest data, the top 20 radio advertisers increased their combined spend on radio by 16.5 % year-on-year, allocating 11.2 % of their total media budgets to radio (see Figure 1.8).

Since 1992, commercial radio advertising revenue has consistently grown faster than the media market as a whole, making radio the fastest growing medium of the last decade (see Figure 1.9).

Rank	Advertiser	MAT July 04	% radio share	% change yr-on-yr
1	COI Communications	£28,605,408	16.3	12.9
2	British Telecom	£10,112,949	11.4	105.6
3	Sainsbury's	£8,360,099	16.9	−11.9
4	Procter & Gamble	£7,872,140	4.1	−18.5
5	Vodafone	£6,263,433	14.1	19.2
6	Hutchinson 3G	£6,127,326	14.2	104
7	Carphone Warehouse	£5,635,459	41.7	176.3
8	Lever Faberge Homecare	£5,490,313	8.7	27.5
9	News International	£5,297,876	13.5	−34.6
10	Orange	£4,922,199	8.1	9.6
11	Camelot	£4,844,527	19.9	6.2
12	Ford	£4,753,266	6.8	−6.7
13	Telewest Communications	£4,693,286	51.4	−22.4
14	Renault	£4,629,541	7.6	5.8
15	Toyota	£4,391,440	8.8	47.8
16	Flextech Telewest	£3,875,545	41.4	93.4
17	British Sky Broadcasting	£3,816,191	7.7	71.7
18	Specsavers	£3,640,927	15.8	32
19	Vauxhall	£3,506,554	5.9	29.9
20	British Airways	£3,057,975	9.6	42.7
	Total	£129,896,454	**11.2%**	**16.5%**

Figure 1.8 Top 20 radio advertisers MAT to July 2004

This growth has also been reflected in radio's overall share of advertising revenue since 1992 – commercial radio achieved a share of 7 % of display advertising revenue for the first time in the MAT to Q1 2004 (see Figure 1.10).

The result of this growth is that radio has finally shaken off its '2 %' tag and been promoted from the position of an 'also ran' to a considered and active media choice competing for major advertisers' media budgets alongside the other mainstream media.

Undoubtedly, radio's growth as a medium has been a key driver in this evolution, but the development of greater understanding of the unique communication qualities and proven results that radio offers to advertisers has also been an important

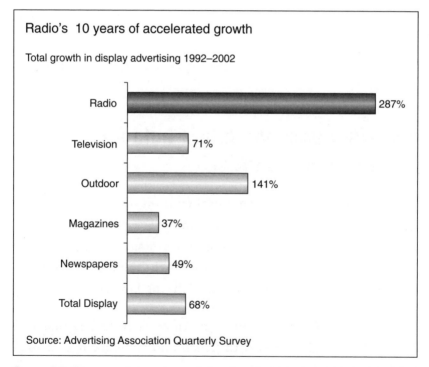

Figure 1.9 The growth in commercial radio advertising revenue compared to other media

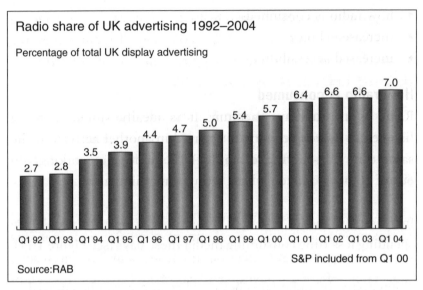

Figure 1.10 Commercial radio's annual share of display advertising

factor. These characteristics are reviewed in greater depth in Chapter 2.

1.5 What does the future hold for commercial radio?

The last 15 years have seen a proliferation of new competitive media channels vying for people's time, yet radio has continued to attract new listeners and maintain average weekly listening hours. But what of the future – how might radio develop in the 21st century and what will be the defining factors?

Our analysis suggests that there are three main factors that will drive further audience growth (reach *and* time spent listening) for radio in the future:

- how radio is consumed;
- increased choice;
- increased accessibility.

How radio is consumed

Radio is an auxiliary medium. It is ideally suited to being listened to by people who are engaged in another activity at the same time (e.g. driving, cleaning, DIY, gardening, working) – 9 out of 10 people listen whilst doing something else.

Increasingly, media research is demonstrating that people are spending less time consuming media these days (see Figure 1.11).

Comparatively, radio fares better – because it can be enjoyed in full whilst doing other things; it is not viewed as a time-drain in the same way as other media. This is probably the reason why

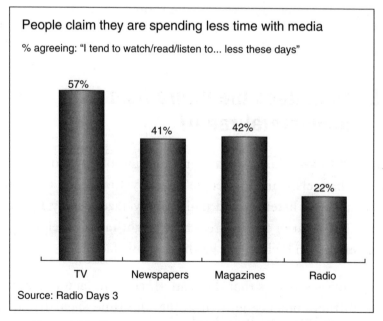

Figure 1.11 Time spent consuming traditional media is falling

radio's share of all time spent with media shows a small increase in recent years, whilst other media are static or in decline, mainly due to the rise of the Internet and more time spent watching DVDs (Figure 1.12).

'Radio's strength is its immense flexibility, adaptability and suitability for a modern and active life. It suits people who move around a lot; it suits people who are busy doing other things'.

Mary Kenny, 'Why the good old wireless still has pulling power', *Daily Express.*

So, even though people are spending less time with media in general and new media are eating into the time people spend with traditional media, radio's status as the one true accompaniment medium suggests that it will continue to hold its own in terms of audience growth in the future.

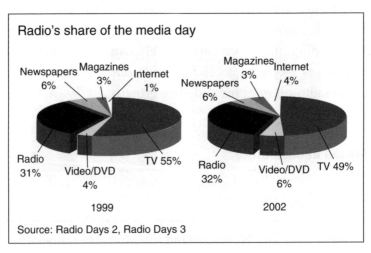

Figure 1.12 Radio's share of the media day

Increased choice

We have already touched on how increased choice of station formats amongst the 274 analogue commercial radio stations has contributed to the steep growth of the commercial radio audience across the last 15 years.

This choice is further augmented by the 130 commercial DAB services that currently exist. These roughly fall into four categories:

* local digital simulcasts of existing analogue services;
* non-local digital simulcasts of local analogue services from other parts of the UK;
* digital-only brands developed by existing radio players (e.g. Capital Disney, Virgin's The Groove, and GWR's Planet Rock);
* digital-only brands developed by industry newcomers (e.g. Abracadabra, Gaydar Radio).

As of mid-2004, DAB receiver penetration stood at about 600 000 sets, so we are yet to see the real benefits of this greater choice on increasing commercial radio listening. But with average prices dropping and more models being made available, DAB penetration is likely to accelerate and contribute more significantly to radio's long-term audience growth.

Increased accessibility

One of the most significant changes in radio over the past couple of years has been the growth in availability of existing analogue radio stations through new platforms. Beyond DAB, digital television (Sky, cable and Freeview) and the Internet offer significant choice to listeners (see Figure 1.13).

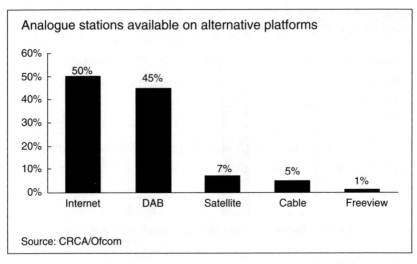

Figure 1.13 Analogue stations available on alternative platforms

Another recent trend has seen radio receivers increasingly incorporated into other devices, such as mobile phones.

These shifts have led to a greater accessibility of the medium, creating new listening situations and occasions that in turn are contributing to greater listening.

The *Internet* is a popular way to listen to the radio, with 7.3 million adults (15 % of the population) tuning in this way (see Figure 1.14).

Young people are the heaviest online radio listeners – about a quarter of all 15–34s access their favourite stations on the web. Frequency of listening via the Internet is also high – just under half of those who tune in online do so at least once a week, whilst 12 % claim to listen every day/most days.

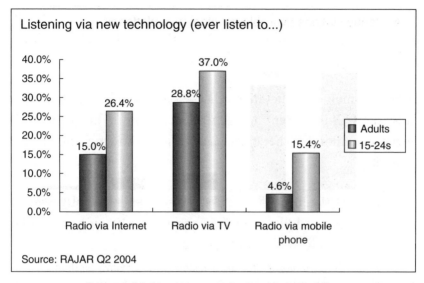

Source: RAJAR Q2 2004

Figure 1.14 Listening to radio via new technology

Internet radio is principally listened to by office workers. This has previously been a difficult audience to reach. The listening pattern is one where we see a peak around lunchtime and another peak towards the end of the working day.

As broadband becomes more popular, providing high-speed Internet access to homes, we can expect to see increased amounts of online listening at home – while children surf on the Internet or do their homework on their PC.

Over half of households in the UK now have a *digital television* service, allowing access to radio stations as well as TV channels. The free-to-view service Freeview has been an important driver in digital television penetration over the last two years, having sold over 3.5 million sets.

The number of adults listening to the radio via the TV currently stands at over 14 million or 28 % of the population (see Figure 1.14).

Younger men are the most likely audience to tune in this way. Growth is evident across all demographics, however, with listening amongst the older age groups showing the fastest growth.

Frequency of listening via the TV is also high, reflecting its ease of use and accessibility – 13 % of those who listen to the radio via the TV claim to tune in every day.

Growth in both the number of listeners and the frequency of listening is expected to continue, along with the rise in multi-channel households. Freeview boxes are often bought as a second digital TV access, usually for use in the bedroom, where radio listening tends to be more commonplace, especially amongst the younger age groups.

Mobile phones with radio receivers are becoming a part of every-day life, increasing opportunities to listen to the radio whilst on the move. Over 2.2 million people in the UK have used their mobile phones to listen to the radio (approximately 5 % of the adult population) – up almost 50 % year-on-year (see Figure 1.14).

Listening via a mobile phone is most prevalent amongst younger and more affluent demographics and those likely to be early adopters of new technology – the latest mobile handsets are now a required accessory for many young people.

We expect this trend to continue as radio receivers become stan-dard in more mobile phone handsets and prices fall, opening up new listening opportunities to more and more listeners.

The three factors of how radio is consumed, increased choice and increased accessibility all suggest that the radio audience will continue to grow, whilst the long-term decline in audiences to other mainstream media will continue.

Perhaps because of these favourable audience predictions, long-term advertising revenue forecasts for commercial radio suggest a faster rate of growth than for the media market as a whole. It appears that the trend of consistent share growth for radio across the last 14 years is set to continue for the foreseeable future.

1.6 Summary

- Commercial radio has made significant strides since it was launched just over thirty years ago.
- There are now 274 analogue and 130 digital stations broadcasting in the UK, at national, regional and local levels. Two-thirds of adults listen every week and the variety of station formats available means that commercial radio is disproportionately successful at attracting a younger audience that is traditionally difficult to reach through other mass media.
- In advertising terms, radio now commands a 7% share of advertising revenue, up from 2.8% in 1992, and is playing an increasingly significant role in the plans of major advertisers such as Unilever, Sainsbury's, P&G, BT and the government (via COI Communications).
- Despite increased competition from a vast array of new media, it is predicted that radio audiences will continue to grow, driven by increased station choice, increased accessibility and the medium's auxiliary qualities.

2
The 'True' Radio Context

This is where we find out what radio is really like as a medium – the way people use it in their daily routines and the role it plays in their emotional lives (which may surprise you).

Radio is famous for 'reaching the parts that other media cannot reach', but how does this work in practice? We take a closer look at niche audiences and modal targeting strategies.

Radio also has nicknames in the media community – 'the intimate medium' and 'the frequency medium' – what do these mean for brands wanting to get the best results?

Finally, how effective is radio? This chapter reviews the research evidence for radio's ability to promote brand awareness and 'shift boxes'.

2.1 Why and how people listen

Why people listen to radio

There are two key facets to listeners' requirements from radio – the first is a functional requirement, while the second is an emotional one.

The functional requirement is the need for information – news, time checks, traffic news, weather or sports results. In a recent RAB research study, one respondent described how listening to the radio could make the difference between her journey to work taking 30 minutes or an hour and a half.

The emotional requirement is characterised by listeners in terms of the relationship they have with either a presenter or a particular music show.

The reality of people's daily patterns is that the two requirements are not mutually exclusive – the balance between them changes across the course of a day according to listeners' moods, with stations being chosen according to the mood of the moment.

'Radio remains a ray of light in the darkness, a loyal friend and companion. Even when listeners are not always aware that they are listening to it'.

Paul Donovan, *The Sunday Times*

How listening requirements change across the day

Breakfast

At breakfast time, the functional element is at its highest. The most successful breakfast presenters are seen by listeners as those that are able to fulfil their functional role as a provider of news, travel, weather, etc., while at the same time providing an emotional feelgood factor – it's not surprising that virtually all radio stations' programming reflects the functional requirement in the morning.

The choice of station is likely to be the same day after day and is probably the one that the radio alarm clock is tuned to. Additionally, breakfast time is when there is most need of consensus in choice of station, since the listening experience is more likely to be shared. Listeners tend to sum up the role of the radio in the morning as 'It's for getting the house up'.

Daytime
During the daytime, radio is used in a classic background mode and listeners see this as a positive attribute. The relationship is uncritical and undemanding, with the result that the medium is used to create the right atmosphere to accompany daytime tasks.

This part of the day sees listeners outside the office making more personal choices of stations from across their repertoire. In contrast, listening in the workplace relies on consensus and leads to more habitual station choice. In qualitative research, people who listen in the office sum up the role of radio during the day as 'keeping the mood just right'.

Evening/weekends
Listening in the evening and at the weekends requires greater commitment on the part of the listener. Given the alternatives, principally television, the decision to turn the radio on is much more conscious and as such the attention and involvement levels during this period are higher.

It is during the evening and at weekends that listeners are most likely to seek out particular music shows by appointment. Radio station programming again reflects this need, with the scheduling of specialist music shows at these times.

Despite the competition of other media choices, radio listening during weekday evenings is growing at a faster rate than any other segment. Beyond a greater interest in the specialist programming, it is believed that an increasing use of radio to accompany Internet usage sessions at home is also contributing to this growth.

The physicality of listening

Most radio listening tends to take place when people are on their own. It is common for radio listening to take place in a personal space such as the bedroom, bathroom, kitchen or car (see Figure 2.1). Because of the solitary/personal nature of listening, in almost all cases the listener is listening to the station that they

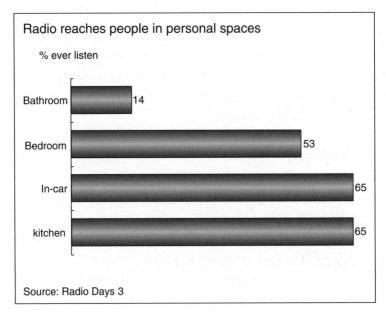

Figure 2.1 Radio reaches people in personal spaces

:ed (once again, compare this with, for example, TV or secondary newspaper/magazine readership).

The vast majority of radio listening occurs at the same time every day, particularly during the working week. People use radio to help them wake up, get ready and get out of the house. A lot of regular listening also occurs in-car on the way to work or during the school run.

This habitual listening behaviour also extends to station selection. Despite the huge proliferation in station choice, people's station repertoires are still relatively limited (the average listener chooses from a repertoire of 2.5 stations).

For the most part (i.e. 9 out of 10 listening situations), radio is an accompaniment for people involved in a primary activity: listening whilst getting ready for work, driving, working, doing homework, surfing the Internet, etc (see Figure 2.2).

This is a unique characteristic of radio – it is the only medium that people can consume as intended whilst involved in other activity. Whilst other media compete as primary media, radio is characterised as being auxiliary – it really is different.

In summary, radio listening can be characterised by five main traits:

- it is solitary;
- it takes place in a personal space;
- station selection is a matter of personal choice;
- listening is habitual and listeners are loyal to their preferred stations;
- radio is auxiliary to other activities.

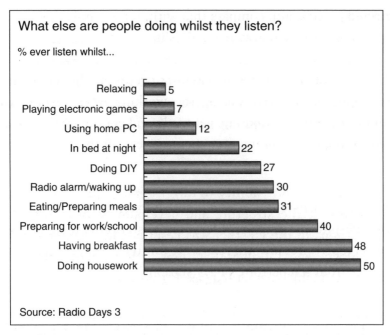

Figure 2.2 Primary activities during which people listen to the radio

2.2 Radio's media attributes

Alongside the structure of the medium, the characteristics of radio listening have a direct influence on the media qualities that radio offers advertisers compared to other media.

We have summarised the main media attributes under the following themes:

- targeting;
- presence;
- outreach.

Each of these is reviewed in more depth below.

Targeting (audiences, modes, moods)

Like some other media, radio is able to offer advertisers the opportunity to target precise *demographic* audiences. However, the nature of most radio listening (as described above) means that, uniquely amongst media, radio can also offer the opportunity to target *local communities, communities of interest, consumer moods and modes*.

In considering radio's ability to target *demographics*, it is valuable to revisit the structure and development of commercial radio stations in the UK that was described in Chapter 1. With 274 analogue and 130 digital stations, it is clear that the radio audience is highly segmented (see Figure 1.6).

This audience segmentation allows advertisers the opportunity to target a specific demographic audience highly efficiently through selective stations, or to reach a mass audience by combining a wide range of stations.

There are many stations which bring together listeners who share a common interest, be it a particular music genre such as classical or rock, jazz or dance music, sports, arts or books. These are often referred to as serving *communities of interest*, examples of which include well-established stations such as Classic FM or Kiss FM, plus newer stations such as Planet Rock and Oneword.

With these stations there is a clear sense of who the listener is, both in terms of demographics and in terms of lifestyle. These stations play a valuable role in the lives of their listeners, keeping them up to date with news and information in their particular area of interest.

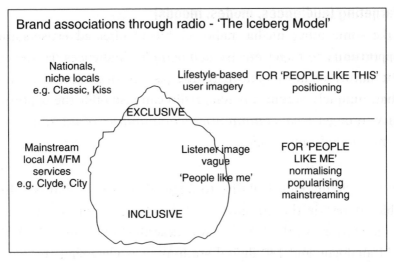

Figure 2.3 Brand associations through radio – the 'Iceberg Model'

These stations are valuable for advertisers aiming to position their brands and associate with a certain lifestyle group (see Figure 2.3).

Radio stations serving *geographical communities* reach those groups of people living or working within a certain area. Hence, they are usually local or regional analogue stations and range from large stations, such as 95.8 Capital FM in London, through to those covering a much smaller local community, such as 2-Ten FM in Reading or Fusion in Lewisham.

Listeners to this type of station tend to represent a broad mix of demographics from the station's catchment area. They are likely to tune in for local news and information, and this can help them feel a sense of belonging to the community in which they live.

Listener image is less clear with these stations, tending to be rather 'mainstream'; listeners feel that the station is broadcast for them and assume that the rest of the audience are also 'people like me', be that old, young, rich or poor. Hence, it is not as easy for 'outsiders' to describe listeners by anything other than where they live.

The media effect of this is to suggest implicitly that brands advertised on these stations are mainstream, contemporary and popular (see Figure 2.3).

Finally, because radio listening is used to accompany other tasks taking place across the day, it is an effective means of targeting consumers when they are operating in a particular *mode*, or are looking to enhance a particular *mood*. As covered in Section 2.1, station content is often designed to fit with the listener's *modus operandi*, providing the ideal context for advertisers to speak to people in this way.

The benefit of this for advertisers is that research demonstrates that advertising recall is higher when the listener is engaged in an activity that relates to an advertised brand (see Figure 2.4).

Whilst it is possible that a similar effect may be achievable with other media, radio is the only medium where nine out of ten of those listening are doing something else at the same time.

Presence

There are several factors that contribute to radio's ability to increase a brand's media 'presence'. The lower cost of radio airtime relative to other media, in particular TV (see Figure 2.16), is an important factor, and this is augmented by the intrinsic media attributes of the medium.

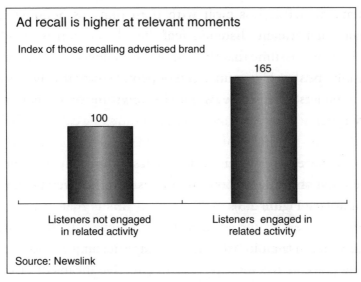

Figure 2.4 *Advertisement recall is higher at relevant moments*

Average weekly frequency for different media	
TV	1–2 OTS (opportunities to see)
Press	1–2 OTS (opportunities to see)
Radio	3–4 OTH (opportunities to hear)

Figure 2.5 Weekly frequency generated by an 'average' campaign in this medium

Radio is often referred to as the *frequency* medium because it naturally builds higher levels of frequency than other mainstream media (e.g. TV, press – see Figure 2.5). This happens even at relatively low rating levels as a result of habitual listening patterns.

So radio allows brands to speak to consumers more regularly than other media. Because radio advertisers are 'on a lot' in a medium that accounts for a high share (a third) of the media day (see Figure 1.12) people often refer to radio as being good at enhancing a brand's *share of mind*.

Many brands seek to gain a competitive advantage in terms of media presence by achieving a higher *share of voice* (i.e. share of media spend) than other advertisers in the same category, believing that this can help enhance a brand's share of mind. Radio is a less mature advertising market than, for example, TV or print media and is therefore less prone to saturation within individual advertiser categories. The result of this is that in most categories it is easier for advertisers to achieve a higher share of voice in radio than in other mainstream media.

As we have already explored, radio is particularly strong in delivering audiences in the morning – in fact it offers the largest audience of any real-time medium across the morning through to the middle of the afternoon (see Figure 2.6). The benefit of this to advertisers is that it can help balance a brand's media *presence across the day*.

This is of particular benefit to advertisers who conform to the *recency* model of advertising. Recency theory is based on two main pillars:

1. Not having an advertising presence is the equivalent of not having product on-shelf.
2. Advertising is more effective if it is closer to the time of action/purchase (the research detailed in Figure 2.4 reinforces this hypothesis).

Radio's ability to generate greater media presence compared to other media (via lower costs, higher frequency), coupled with its ability to reach people as they prepare their shopping list or when

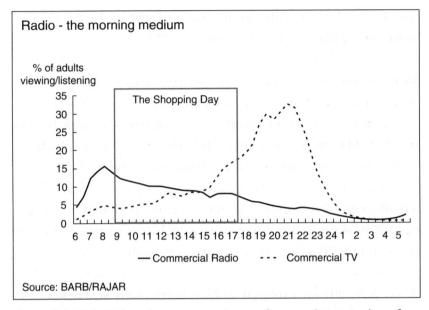

Figure 2.6 Radio offers the largest audience of any real-time medium from morning to mid-afternoon

they are in-car on the way to the shops, make it ideally suited to recency advertisers in the grocery sector. But the benefits of recency radio aren't just limited to grocery brands – reaching people before they go to work in the morning is also important to brands seeking to stimulate response from consumers to a website or phone number.

Outreach

Radio elapses in real time and listeners have to sit through as an advertisement runs its course (zapping is very uncommon on radio – see advertising avoidance point below).

This means that as radio listeners we are obliged to deal with messages from advertisers regardless of whether we are interested in buying the product (this is also true of TV and cinema). Hence, radio is often referred to as an *intrusive* medium. With print media, by contrast, consumers edit ruthlessly according to their own needs and interests.

The intrusive nature of radio is reiterated in research that demonstrates how radio benefits from *low advertising avoidance* levels compared to TV and print media (see Figure 2.7).

These factors combine to make radio good at ensuring that the self-determined *out-of-market* audience is exposed in detail to the brand message (see Figure 2.8). So radio is a great way of reaching out to people and getting them to engage with new ideas, particularly if the advertising is speaking to non-users or rejectors of the brand.

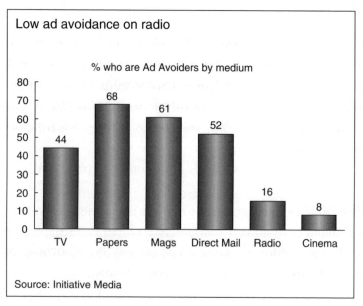

Figure 2.7 Low advertising avoidance on radio

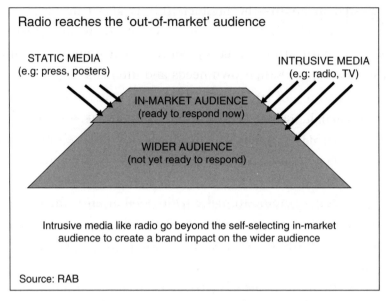

Figure 2.8 Radio reaches the 'out-of-market' audience

'Radio allows you to communicate offers to people who are in the market to buy a phone in the next few weeks, but similarly does a big job in just establishing your brand and some ideas about you in the minds of people who are not in the market right now, but are likely to be sometime in the future.'

Charles Dunstone, Carphone Warehouse

With its ability to reach out-of-market consumers, coupled with lower media costs than TV or cinema, radio is increasingly being seen as a valuable means of alerting consumers to new brand offers and driving response through other media. This use of radio as an *indirect response* medium is explored further in the Career Development Loans case study in Section 2.4.

2.3 How radio communicates

Radio stations are seen as having a positive role in people's lives – keeping them company, giving them information and allaying feelings of loneliness or isolation. The increasing numbers of people working from home or living alone, have led radio to be described as an important 'solitude management' tool.

Habitual listening, combined with the emotional support role that radio plays, means that listeners develop quite a close relationship with their favourite station, as demonstrated in Figure 2.9.

Quantitative research reiterates perceptions of radio as a friend, relative to other media (Figure 2.10).

'Radio is really powerful because it's like personal advocacy, it's like a friend in the pub saying "have you seen?", "you should try", "what about?" There's a certain glossiness to television that takes the advertising a step away from you – with radio it's like a recommendation from a friend'.

Katrina Lowes, BT

"If my radio station were a person..."

"a friend"
"someone you would talk to in the pub"
"someone fun"
"lively"
"take him home to meet mum"
"a mate" / "a companion"

Figure 2.9 If your radio station came to life and walked into the room, what kind of person would that be?

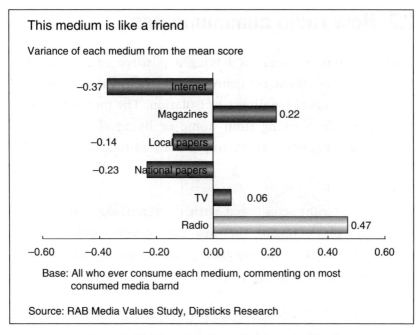

Figure 2.10 The perception of radio as 'a friend'

Perhaps because of this 'friend' relationship between station and listener, consumers hold particularly high levels of trust in radio compared with some other media (Figure 2.11).

So listeners tune into radio for emotional reasons; to provide a friendly voice to help lift their mood when they are engaged in other tasks. But what are the implications of this relationship for radio advertising?

One of the main challenges that advertising faces on radio is *zoning*. Levels of advertising avoidance on radio are low, but as Figure 2.12 demonstrates, listeners' attention is clearly not focused onto radio output all the time. Indeed, one of the reasons why radio listening is so popular is that it does not require constant attention.

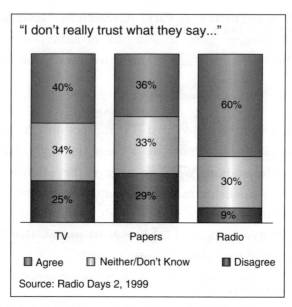

Figure 2.11 'I don't really trust what they say on TV/in the papers/on radio'

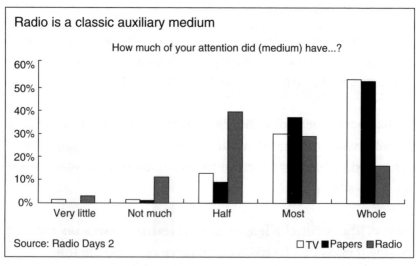

Figure 2.12 Percentage attention given by people to various media

But how does attentiveness vary? Research by Navigator established that listeners 'zone in and out' of radio – regardless of whether the output is music, news, weather, advertisements, competitions, etc.

So what draws people in? Whilst it is not possible to create universal rules on attentiveness, it is clear that radio has to rely heavily on the spoken word to engage the attention of the listener. And whilst that may make radio appear simple to write for, the sensitive nature of the listener's ear (as demonstrated in the Megalab Truth Test in Figure 2.13) means that they are highly critical of how things come across.

In 1995, *Nature* magazine featured the results of a study into the way people deal with lies – the 'Megalab Truth Test'. The purpose of the test was to analyse the way people were influenced by verbal, visual and vocal clues in detecting lies. Political commentator Sir Robin Day was interviewed twice about his

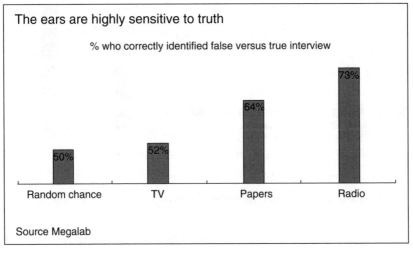

Figure 2.13 The results of the Megalab Truth Test

favourite films: in one interview he consistently told the truth, in the other he consistently lied. The interviews were published in the press, broadcast on TV and played out on radio, and people were asked to phone in and say which interview contained the lies.

Over 40 000 people took part, and the results, by medium, are shown in Figure 2.13. They suggest very strongly that when people are listening (with no visual cues) they are significantly more able to tell when lies are being told.

The fact that the ears are sensitive to honesty fits with what consumers sometimes say about bad radio advertising – that the voices sound 'artificial' or that the actors are 'pretending'.

This suggests two requirements in radio creativity:

1. If you ask your announcer to be unbelievably enthusiastic about your product, then, sure enough, people are unlikely to believe him/her; consider a more genuine approach.
2. If you want listeners to believe your characters enough to 'zone in' on what they're saying, you will need to ensure you have good actors, good direction and enough studio time to find out what works.

Brand image vs. Brand character

Analysis of successful radio campaigns from the past leads us to conclude that radio is different in one important respect from the visual advertising media – it doesn't deal in brand image, it deals in brand character (Figure 2.14).

It's a fairly subtle difference, and both are components of the wider concept of brand personality, but they represent different

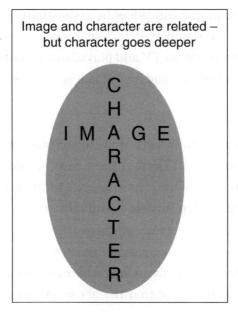

Figure 2.14 Brand image vs. brand character

ways of knowing the brand (or, from the advertiser's point of view, of manipulating the brand).

Radio is good at brand character because it doesn't speak the language of image (which is largely a visual concept). It doesn't use glossy, aspirational imagery and it speaks with a human voice.

Communicating at brand character level is very important for brands that seek to build a closer relationship with the consumer. Brand character comes over strongly in radio advertising, especially as an expression of the brand's attitude towards the listener (or, in listener's language, 'how they come across').

2.4 Effectiveness of the medium

There are various levels at which advertising effectiveness can be interpreted by advertisers – see Figure 2.15.

Over recent years, the radio industry has invested significant resource into demonstrating the effectiveness of radio in delivering against these different measures of success. This has helped advertisers to feel more confident in investing in the medium and has been an important driver in helping radio to build share against the other mainstream media.

The *Awareness Multiplier*, conducted by Millward Brown and published in 2000, focused on radio's ability to generate advertising *awareness*. This showed that radio was three-fifths as effective as TV on average, but at one-seventh of the price –

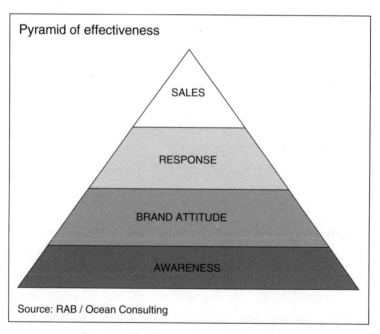

Figure 2.15 The pyramid of effectiveness

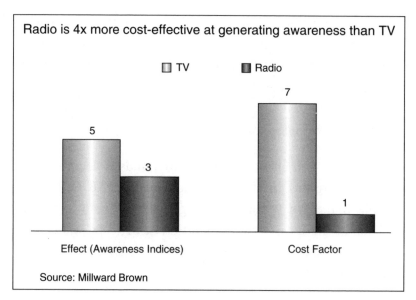

Figure 2.16 Radio is four times more cost effective at generating awareness than TV

making radio therefore potentially four times as cost-effective (see Figure 2.16).

It also demonstrated the 'multiplier effect' – that the effectiveness of a TV budget could be improved by as much as 15 %, simply by redeploying 10 % onto radio.

There has also been extensive work on radio's ability to drive direct response. The most important study in this area was the joint GWR/BT/DMA study of telephone *response* in the mid-nineties, which demonstrated how widely response rates varied for different brands.

More interesting are the case studies that demonstrate how radio works as an *indirect response* medium, i.e. driving greater response through other media. In the campaign for Career Development Loans (developed by COI Communications on behalf of the Department for Employment), radio was added on a regional basis to a national schedule of press inserts. In the regions where radio was used, awareness of the loans doubled and response to the press inserts was 60 % higher than in the non-radio regions. It was concluded that radio advertising created a climate of awareness and interest in the offer within which response to the press inserts was accelerated.

The way radio can change *attitudes* to brands is documented in many case studies in the RAB database at RAB OnLine: for example Marston's Pedigree, Kellogg's Nutri-Grain and Listerine. Each of these case studies is different in scope and content, and it's not possible to devise averages in terms of changing brand perceptions.

In terms of *sales*, The Sales Multiplier study conducted by dunnhumby demonstrated that across a range of 17 brands, the average sales uplift attributable to radio was 9 % (see Figure 2.17). The average uplift for each 100 radio gross rating points (GRPs) was 2.2 %.

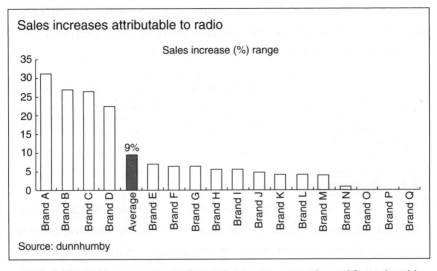

Figure 2.17 Across a range of 17 brands, the average sales uplift attributable to radio was 9 %

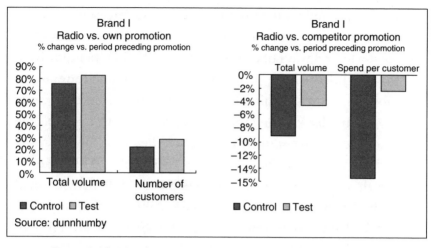

Figure 2.18 How radio advertising works with price promotions

It also demonstrated that radio advertising augmented the positive effects of a brand's price promotion and helped offset the negative effects of a competitor's price promotion on a brand's sales (Figure 2.18).

The wealth of evidence demonstrating radio's effectiveness has helped to shift advertisers' belief in, and subsequently attitudes towards, the medium. Nowadays, if an advertiser tests the medium and doesn't see any positive shifts in their chosen measures, they are more likely to interrogate *their usage* of radio (to understand how they can get it to work better), rather than dismiss the medium as ineffective for their brand. This topic is explored further in Chapter 3.

2.5 Summary

- Radio is primarily used by listeners to help lift their mood when they are on their own, engaged in other tasks. It is a unique medium in that it can be consumed as intended whilst the listener is involved in another primary activity.

- Whilst this offers brands valuable communication opportunities, it also means that with radio the advertiser is challenged to find ways of engaging the listener in what they have to say whilst leaving them with a positive brand impression.
- Most listening is habitual, occurring at the same time every day, particularly during the working week, with many people using radio to accompany them when they wake up, get ready and get out of the house. During these times, the medium can also play a functional role, keeping the audience informed of the latest news, travel information and weather forecast.
- These characteristics of listening, alongside the structure of the medium, influence the media qualities that radio offers advertisers.
- Radio offers many efficient targeting possibilities, including niche demographic audiences, local communities, communities of interest, consumer moods and modes.
- Radio is able to extend a brand's media presence in terms of frequency and share of voice, reaching consumers across the whole day. These qualities are considered particularly valuable within the context of the 'recency' model of advertising.
- As a real-time medium, radio is effective at reaching out to consumers who aren't yet in the market to buy, and leaving them with a persuasive impression of a brand.
- Radio's effectiveness as an advertising medium in terms of driving awareness, sales and response has been proven in a series of wide-ranging research studies. Individual case studies also demonstrate radio's ability to shift the listener's attitude towards a brand.

3
The Need for a Different Approach

How often does it happen that you hear a radio campaign for a brand you admire and wonder why it is speaking to you in such an irritating way? It's too common – and it's not just a UK problem.

The answer lies partly in a misunderstanding of the way radio communicates, and partly in outdated working practices.

This chapter takes a closer look at the realities of radio communication, and why the 'conversational' nature of radio as a medium may hold the key to successful campaign strategies.

3.1 Why the need for a different approach?

Advertising is constantly having to adapt to maintain its effectiveness – we see this in the growth of innovations in all media, such as red button usage in digital TV and lenticular sites in outdoor advertising. These are examples of ways that media innovations can help brands to find new ways to connect with people – more effective ways than the well-trodden orthodoxies of the past.

But this is where radio is a little bit different. With radio, we are not in a situation where we have learned to exploit the maximum the medium has to offer: we are not just looking for innovations to help us take this further. The reality with radio is that we are only just learning how to exploit it in its basic form.

Consider the ads that you hear on radio day-to-day. What percentage of them could you describe as expertly crafted, confident in their creative use of the medium, sure-footedly exploiting the power of the airwaves? Not many.

How many of them leave you with an impression about the brand which is stimulating, distinctive, memorable or engaging? Fewer still.

'I think there is a kind of built-in expectation that radio commercials must be funny. I think it's a shame . . . the commercials that sometimes stand out on the radio are the ones which aren't a two-handed comedy ending with a lame joke – which seems to be the classic formula.'

David Abbott (creative)

And don't be fooled into thinking it's only little local brands that lack this expertise. Some of the biggest brands on the planet, using the highest-regarded agencies in the world, lack confidence when it comes to radio (this is not just a UK finding – radio industries across the developed world report similar issues). We take a closer look at the reasons why in Section 3.3.

'The quality of radio advertising is improving – I think – but I don't think we have the confidence with radio that we do with other media.'

Jo Kenrick (advertiser)

'We must take more care with radio, because the reality is this: people will hear us.'

David Abbott (creative)

'Radio is a challenging medium for creatives. It demands a certain way of thinking that is different from the visual media.'

Robert Campbell (creative)

'If big agencies were good at radio, we wouldn't have built up Radioville as a successful business, and we wouldn't have national brands on our client list.'

Adrian Reith (creative)

But before we proceed, a question arises. Are we in danger of being precious? Why does radio advertising actually have to be 'creative'?

3.2 Why does radio advertising have to be creative?

There are two answers to this question. One is about whether your advertising is noticed and remembered (i.e. recall), the other is about the kind of impression you create for your brand.

Role in recall

There is copious evidence that creativity affects recall in all sorts of advertising media, and in radio there is one study that is particularly useful in this regard – the RAB's *Awareness Multiplier* study.

This was conducted by Millward Brown in 2000, and tracked the advertising awareness of seventeen brands (mix of retail and fmcg brands) in test and control areas in the Midlands area of the UK. Consumers were exposed to the same levels of advertising in all media except radio, where geography allowed Millward Brown to divide them into listeners and non-listeners: this allowed the effect of radio to be identified (for more information and advice on measuring the effect of radio, see Chapter 6).

The study was actually set up to measure the effectiveness of radio compared with TV. It showed that radio was three-fifths as effective as TV at raising advertising awareness, but that this was achieved at one-seventh of the price; so one important conclusion of the study was that radio is, on average, about four times as cost-effective as TV.

However, some radio campaigns were far more effective than others – see Figure 3.1. The top scoring campaign, with an Awareness Index of 6, was 500 % more efficient than the lowest scorer – a very significant difference.

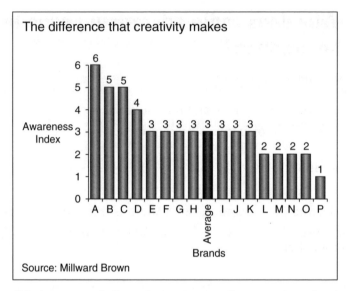

Figure 3.1 Awareness indices for various radio campaigns in the RAB Awareness Multiplier study

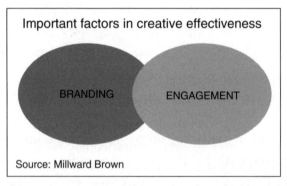

Figure 3.2 Important factors in creative effectiveness

Millward Brown analysed the reasons for the difference. They identified (see Figure 3.2) that the highest performing ads in the test were characterised by good branding (i.e. a strong linkage with the brand being advertised) and high levels of engagement (i.e. something about the ad that makes the audience listen rather than zone out).

If branding and engagement are the crucial factors for maximising effective recall, this is a task for the creative work.

Role in brand impression

In the seminars run by the Radio Advertising Bureau, the question sometimes arises – 'how can we say that irritating ads are bad if they make people go out and buy the product? They may be annoying or patronising, but they must be effective, otherwise companies wouldn't run them!'

Or, more prosaically, 'maybe they're not creative – but you remember them!'

You probably know the ads meant here – they tend to be very unsubtle attempts to get the listener to remember the brand name or the telephone number, or just plain boring, predictable commercials which are repeated ad nauseam. Or the jokes which were first written in 1972 and can be seen coming from about a mile off.

Yes, those ads often do work, if 'work' is limited simply to short-term issues such as creating awareness, driving store-traffic, generating phone calls and stimulating purchase. It's common to find local radio listeners can spontaneously recall the jingle for a local trader who has been on radio – even if they really dislike it.

But where they don't work is in building a longer-term success for the brand: they create a brand which is seen as annoying, patronising and uninterested in the feelings of its customers.

It has famously been said that brands are like people, so we're talking about the equivalent of being remembered as a person who is annoying, patronising and disliked.

For some brands, in the short term, this doesn't really matter. For example, if you just have to sell 5000 mattresses because you are closing down the business, who cares if people are irritated by your ads?

But in the long term it creates a brand that nobody wants to know – and in a world where the difference between a winning brand and a losing brand is in brand perceptions, this is vital. Successful brands have many friends.

3.3 Why aren't we better at using radio?

There are many reasons why we are not more confident in using radio as an advertising medium. Some relate to skills, some to orthodoxies, or received wisdom, in the ad business. Here are the main factors.

Radio is too good at last-minute tactical campaigns

Everyone in the business knows that radio campaigns can be turned round in a very short time, and at relatively low cost, and this makes it an ideal medium for the marketer who wants to do something late and unplanned – so quality tends to go out of the window. It's famously been said for projects that, out of Quick, Cheap and Good, you can have any two but rarely three (Figure 3.3).

The radio skills shortage

Creatives in advertising often come from a graphic arts back-ground, which is not relevant to radio. There are radio courses available (see www.aerialsfoundation.co.uk) but creatives don't usually see radio as an area where improving their skills will advance their career – it's a fact of life that radio recordings won't usually take them on fabulous trips to Cape Town.

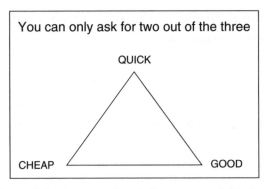

Figure 3.3 You can only ask for two out of the three

It's important to note that radio skills extend way beyond writing: production and direction can make a significant difference and are often overlooked or given to junior agency producers with little or no radio training.

There are client radio skills as well. It's not particularly easy to judge a radio idea on paper, and experience is needed. Clients also have a vital role to play in enabling the best possible results, and in giving permission for the studio process to allow for some magic (for more on this, see Section 5.3).

Not taking radio seriously

This is probably the biggest factor of all, as there are many award-winning and effective campaigns from the past which were created by relatively unskilled people (we will spare their blushes) – but the point is, they took the radio challenge seriously.

This means putting thought into the briefing (not just adding the word 'radio' onto an existing brief). It means deciding exactly what effect the radio is supposed to achieve – making it much easier to deliver excellent creative work (and much easier for clients to approve that work).

It also means investing enough time and money in the process – and this is specifically an issue for the client – so that people involved can rise to the challenges of the medium.

'Radio is invariably described as blind . . . (yet) whilst paintings, posters and photographs lack sound, their silence ordinarily goes unnoticed.'

Shingler and Wieringa, *On Air: Methods and Meanings of Radio*

3.4 The challenges and opportunities of the medium

'You can say the right thing about a product and nobody will listen. You've got to say it in such a way that people feel it in their gut. Because if they don't feel it, nothing will happen.'

Bill Bernbach (creative)

In the past, radio sometimes had the nickname of 'cheap TV without the pictures', which suggested that the two media were otherwise very similar. We have learned that this is far from the truth.

As we described in detail in Section 2.3, radio is consumed differently, attentiveness to the medium works differently, and it plays a unique role in consumers' lives. The advertiser who understands this context is far better placed to run radio campaigns that make the most of the medium. So what do these factors mean for using the medium better creatively?

Frequency (repetition)

It is an orthodoxy of media planning that listeners are exposed to radio campaigns, on average, about four times more often than campaigns in the press or on TV.

This is why radio ads can become more quickly repetitive, and why multiple copy is essential for any medium-to-heavyweight campaigns.

Conversely, it also means that campaigns rarely go unnoticed, and that ads which were missed or half-heard the first time are sure to be heard again.

Zoning, not zapping

Radio listeners are selective about what they listen to – this is true for news, weather, chat and phone-ins as much as for advertising. They listen to things that interest them or engage their attention for some reason. If there is nothing that engages their mind, they tend to let the output 'go in one ear and come out the other'.

This is very different from TV. There is far less zapping between channels during ad breaks, and in fact there is far less sense of a 'break' for advertising: on TV, the ads tend to be seen as interruptions in the flow of an identifiable programme or film, whereas on radio, ads are part of a flow of different items – talk, news, music tracks, etc.

This makes position-in-break less of an issue with radio: items of output are attended to in turn. Equally, it means that unless an ad has some kind of engaging content, it is in danger of being ignored.

The intimacy of radio

Radio is often called 'the intimate medium', and this is because of the way it is consumed. People tend to listen on their own, in personal spaces such as the kitchen, bathroom or the car.

They also use radio to affect their mood – to alleviate feelings of loneliness or boredom, or to feel more connected with the world.

This gives the radio advertiser access to a very unusual area of people's lives – the intimate area.

The invasiveness of radio

In a sense, this is the flip side of radio's intimacy. If a listener is alone in their kitchen, trying to unwind at the end of a stressful day, a commercial which comes over as hectoring or patronising is unwelcome – but rather difficult to ignore. This intrusiveness is true of both TV and radio (both real-time media, whereas ads in static media like newspapers can easily be ignored), but is particularly acute with radio because of the intimate listening situation and the low levels of station-switching.

This puts the onus on the advertiser to attune their creative work to ensure it is respectful of the listener.

The 'conversational' nature of radio

When you put all these aspects of radio together, they add up to defining its 'conversational' nature. Listening to the radio is not a conspicuous activity for which one dedicates time during the day. Rather, it is something that one does as part of a habitual routine – but a routine which is constantly about renewing and refreshing, bringing new information and stimulation into one's personal space.

This is important for thinking about how radio advertising works. For example, it is common for poster advertising to seek to be arresting – something that stops you in your tracks (through shock tactics perhaps, or being close to the line of decency). If advertising on a 'conversational' medium behaves in this way, there seems to be a misfit. A conversation which is repeated, invasive, intimate and uses shock tactics sounds potentially unpleasant. This may begin to explain why some seemingly great ideas on paper, sound terrible when heard on a radio station.

It also begins to suggest how expert radio advertising might begin to harness the true power of the conversational medium.

3.5 Summary

- As an industry, the communications business has not yet mastered radio in the way it has other media. This is true internationally, and is true for big global brands as well as for small local businesses.
- Creativity is essential because it can make a proven 500 % difference to the memorability of advertising messages.
- Creativity is also the critical component in brand impression. If a campaign (in any medium) makes a negative impression – seeming patronising, hectoring or silly – this influences brand perceptions.
- Radio advertising quality is hampered by various factors – there is a skills shortage in the advertising business, but the biggest barrier is the fact that radio is not taken seriously. It is seen as easy, cheap, marginal.
- Radio has a unique set of challenges and opportunities:
  — ads are repeated more often in radio than other media;

— listener attention varies – they 'zone in and out' according to their interest;

— listening is an intimate experience;

— ads can be seen as invasive in this intimate context.

- Radio is essentially 'conversational' – this militates against approaches that seek to startle or boast, and encourages approaches where brands seek to relate to consumers at a human level.

SECTION 2
HARNESSING THE
TRUE POWER
OF RADIO

In this section we introduce the concept of advanced level radio creativity, and demonstrate how advertisers who take a more active role across the creative development process can achieve this. We suggest both 'marshalling' and 'climate control' techniques to help achieve this.

Chapter 4   What is Advanced Level Creativity?
- Effectiveness is a relative term
- Three common structural problems
- The crucial importance of brand linkage
- Realism vs. shooting for the moon
- Thinking at campaign level
- Summary

Chapter 5   Best Practice Process for Creating Better Radio
- Providing the optimum radio brief
- Judging good radio ideas
- The art of radio production
- Branding in sound
- Summary

Chapter 6   Measuring Radio's Effect
- Defining the research objectives
- The importance of split samples
- Where to do the research
- When to do the research
- Sample sizes
- Method and questionnaire
- Measuring the short-term sales effects of radio
- Measuring the effect of radio sponsorships and promotions
- Summary

4
What is Advanced Level Creativity?

You want your radio advertising to be more creative – the benefits are proven. But what does this actually mean?

As the client, you will be asked to judge the creative proposals, so you need to know what you are talking about. How do you make sure that creativity works effectively on behalf of the brand? How do you avoid advertising which, listeners say, 'goes in one ear and comes out of the other'? Equally, how do you avoid advertising which is 'too creative'?

This chapter takes a closer look at the elements of creative radio advertising, and discusses how they can be used together to achieve optimum results for your campaigns.

4.1 Effectiveness is a relative term

The term 'advertising effectiveness' is often used in daily conversations as if it is a binary concept – the ad worked, or the ad didn't work.

The evidence suggests that this is the wrong way to think about effectiveness. It's clear from the results of the Millward Brown *Awareness Multiplier* study (reviewed in Section 3.2), the dunnhumby *Sales Multiplier* study and the AC Nielsen *Single Source PLUS Radio* study in Germany, that brands in an advertising test will achieve a range of scores – some are basically far more efficient than others (see Figures 3.1, 4.1 and 4.2).

If a piece of advertising (in any medium) is on briefly, it will have some effect – the argument is about how strong that effect is, and the quality of effect in terms of communication.

This may seem a self-evident truth, but in our experience it's worth clarifying, because the advertising industry is inclined to dismiss 'ads that don't work'.

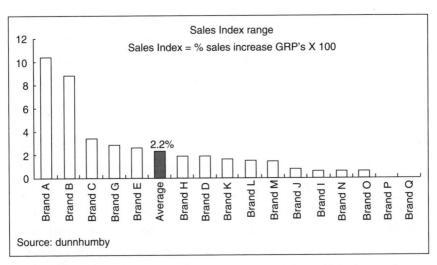

Figure 4.1 Sales index range in the dunnhumby Sales Multiplier study

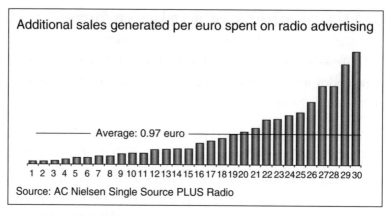

Figure 4.2 Variation in the short-term return on investment

4.2 Three common structural problems

In our workshops with advertisers and agencies we have identified three structural problems that radio commercials sometimes have, which stop them from performing better.

Disconnection from brand/message

Advertising ideas can sometimes work well by being oblique,
and radio is no different from other media in this. But oblique
ideas must resolve in the listener's mind in a way which links
to the brand/message, otherwise there may be little or no connection to the brand/message.

For example, if the advertising brief says 'don't do anything until
you've checked out our latest offers', there is an obvious creative
route that features people not doing anything. But ads which
take this kind of approach have to be extremely well written and
produced, since they require the listener to do a lot of mental
work – link the execution to the message, and then the message
to the brand and its own message.

Disconnection happens when an oblique advertising idea is too uninteresting or weakly presented for listeners to make this effort. This is a greater risk with radio than TV, because TV can use additional visual prompts to shore up the connection (e.g. using the brand logo).

'It's not uncommon to hear a radio ad – even an award-winning one – which is original and funny, but where the brand seems to have gone AWOL.'

Guy Philipson (advertiser)

'Advertising should avoid over-complication, but with radio, the threshold for getting over-complicated is much lower. There is no second sense available to act as a safety net for the confused.'

Ralph van Dijk (creative)

Millward Brown have a useful structural analysis in their LINKtest for pre-testing commercials (see Figure 4.3). Their hypothesis is that ads in the end have three basic structural components:

- the brand or advertiser (this must be included in the memory of the ad, otherwise there will be no effect on the brand);
- the message that the advertising is trying to get across, which may be detailed or simple;
- finally, the creative idea, or the thing in the advertising which engages the consumer in the first place.

The hypothesis is that if any one of these three components is too loosely connected to the other two, the effectiveness of the ad is seriously undermined.

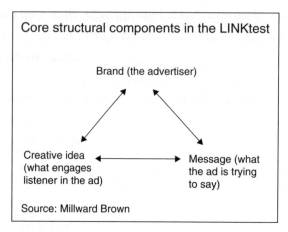

Figure 4.3 Core structural components in the LINKtest

The most common disconnected ads in radio are the ones where the creative idea is too loosely linked to both the message and the brand.

'Sounding like a radio ad'

We in the ad business may feel that ads are a subject of endless fascination – but of course most consumers see them as fairly uninteresting. Sometimes ads can be very entertaining, or striking, or personally resonant, but on the whole, people's expectations of them are pretty low.

If this is true for advertising in general, it's even truer for radio. So when an ad comes on which 'just sounds like a radio ad', people's expectations have already dropped.

Factors identifying such a radio ad would include: over-excited voices, people pretending to be having a conversation but clearly just reading words out, voices gabbling very complicated text, use of marketing jargon such as 'exciting range of offers'.

'If the listener knows what is coming next, they stop caring. And if they don't really care, they don't really listen.'

Adrian Reith (creative)

'The average radio ad isn't usually any fun to listen to; so if your ad sounds like a normal radio ad, why will anyone listen to it?'

Martin Sims (creative)

'People listen to what interests them . . . and sometimes it's a radio commercial.'

Dick Orkin (creative)

Ideas that aren't 'radio-interesting'

Some advertising ideas are difficult to translate from one medium to another. Very verbal ideas can be difficult to execute successfully on posters, very visual ideas can be hard to adapt for radio. Each medium brings its own challenges.

It is difficult to describe the kind of ideas that do work on radio – although radio does seem to thrive on story, on human truth and on surprise.

It is easier to identify approaches that don't work on radio. There is one particular approach in radio advertising that may seem appealing as a concept, but actually is difficult to make engaging on radio, and this is sometimes called the 'journey into sound' or 'soundscapes'. It's often said that radio can take the listener absolutely anywhere – the surface of the moon, the inside of a heart, the middle of a civil war – but the challenge for the creative is to make these journeys interesting enough for the listener to come with them. That is the challenging element.

We were recently shown a script which was set in a vast silent desert, where the vastness and silence were supposed to be engaging. Sure enough, radio can create these scenarios, but the truth is that a vast silent desert is not an inherently interesting place: something has to be happening in the commercial for the listener to project themselves into that place.

'The listener is the art director.'

David Bernstein (creative)

'Have you noticed there aren't any long car chases in books?'

Eddie Izzard (comedian)

4.3 The crucial importance of brand linkage

As we saw in Section 3.2, Millward Brown identified brand linkage as one of the two most important factors in effective advertising. This finding is backed up by other recent studies, and this underlines the critical importance of the area.

The RAB 'research bus'

Passengers on the research bus (see Appendix 1 for details) were all exposed to the test commercials twice in the half-hour journey, yet some commercials were generating less than half the branded recall of others – the recall of the brand was quite independent of recalling the ad.

The IMAS psychometer tests (Germany)

In these tests, the two key variables (see Figure 4.4) are the ability to attract attention (or impact), and content/resonance –

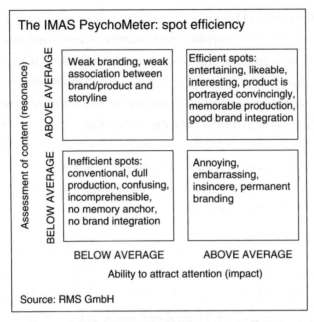

Figure 4.4 The IMAS PsychoMeter: spot efficiency

brands that scored low on this latter criterion were likely to have 'weak branding and a weak chain of association between brand/ product and storyline'.

Brand linkage can make a huge difference to effectiveness, and there are many ways in which brand linkage can be executed – and yet sometimes radio ads rely purely on the brand being mentioned in the ad.

This is not to say that brand linkage needs to be achieved at any price. Listeners soon become uncomfortable with ads that try too hard to make them remember a brand name – this kind of over-insistence can create a kind of desperate tone for the brand (although listen to the Opel Corsa ad at www.better-radio-advertising.co.uk for a canny musical approach).

Alternative models

While the two key attributes of effective radio advertising do appear to be branding and engagement, there will always be exceptions that prove the rule. One famous example is the historic Carphone Warehouse advertising (featured on www.better-radio-advertising.co.uk). This company is famous for having built its brand on radio, but actually the original format for the advertising – an announcement read out over a musical soundbed – relied entirely on relevance to engage attention, while the music did all the brand linking work.

People who were in the market for a mobile phone (or about to enter the market) were more likely to listen to the detail of the product offer, while those outside the market mainly registered the music and the brand name, with a vague memory of the product offer.

For a brand at that life-stage – seeking to establish itself with positive awareness in a market where there were no dominant rivals – this strategy worked extremely well.

4.4 Realism vs. shooting for the moon

If you listen to some of the ads on the CD with this book – Apple Tango 'Lost Property' is a good example – you will realise that these are exceptional ads meeting exceptional briefs. If your brand can offer briefs like these – opportunities to do something really different and 'shoot for the moon' creatively – that's great . . . but it's unusual (see Figure 4.5).

Most of the time, radio ads have to earn their living by promoting offers, reminding people of product benefits, persuading

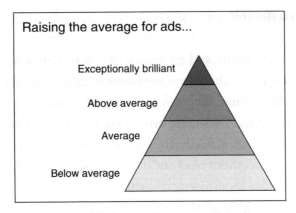

Figure 4.5 Raising the average for ads

people about brand superiority and so on – hard-working, 50-weeks-a-year coalface advertising.

They also have to achieve this at relatively short notice, and under the customary business pressure in terms of budget.

In this context, it is not fair to expect your advertising agency to come up with Apple Tango *'Lost Property'* for every brief.

However, this doesn't mean that advertisers should leave creativity behind. We know that creativity can make commercials more memorable and more effective, so the challenge is to leave room for creativity, even on days where 'shooting for the moon' just isn't possible because of time and money.

Exactly what this means will be looked at in more depth in Chapter 5.

4.5 Thinking at campaign level

Advanced level radio isn't about creating and airing one brilliant commercial. The way radio advertising works is through ongoing contact with the listener – the advertiser's message inveigling its way into listeners' lives over time in a variety of disguises.

This is how campaigns work, and as an advertiser, it is important to think at this level. This means considering the following questions.

How often will my ads be heard?

If the campaign is running at a heavy weight, it is essential that multiple copy is used – the more different executions used, the less repetitive the campaign will feel to the listener. This thinking about multiple copy needs to be included in the early planning for the campaign.

How often will I be on air across the year?

A continuing presence on radio is a powerful tool for the marketer – the combination of frequency and low ad avoidance means that brands can use radio to create a disproportionately large share of mind amongst their customers. But this means the brand will probably need a campaign vehicle of some kind – an agreed approach to advertising which can be adapted each week to accommodate the new message. This is the classic retailer's template – retaining the same basic structure (which is often a brand spokesman) and adapting it as often as required.

4.6 Summary

- Every radio commercial has an effect, but some have a much greater effect than others. There are common structural problems found in radio commercials at the lower end of the effectiveness scale – some of these relate to listener engagement and some to brand linkage, both identified as important factors in radio creative effectiveness.

- Disconnection between idea and brand, sounding like other ads, and ideas that aren't radio friendly have all been identified as factors that can hinder listener engagement in radio ads, and recognition of which brand is speaking to them.

- Strong brand linkage in radio advertising is often overlooked or misunderstood as a vital component in effectiveness (more on this in Section 5.4).

- Advanced level creativity is about being realistic about what you can achieve at a campaign level, and avoiding the common structural problems to produce engaging radio advertising that will deliver business results.

5
Best Practice Process for Creating Better Radio

If radio is more difficult than it looks, the difference lies in the process. In theory, radio is very simple – some words spoken by actors, sound effects, music. . . . But it's in the process that the biggest mistakes can be made, and the greatest improvements brought in.

This chapter looks at the process from start to finish – from briefing through to production – to identify the areas where the pressure points occur, and where you as a client can make the biggest difference.

Each area is summarised with tips, rather than in one large summary at the end of the chapter.

5.1 Providing the optimum radio brief

At the 2004 RAB Advertiser Conference, the delegates were asked about factors they believed were hindering radio creativity – the most common response was 'There isn't enough thinking invested in the radio brief'. The delegates also prioritised 'Briefing' as the most important part of the radio creative development process and the area in which they are most able to make a positive contribution.

So, clearly, briefing is perceived to be a highly important part of the process in achieving a higher level of creativity. Therefore, it seems sensible to spend time considering how to deliver an optimum radio brief. But what are the key elements of the brief for radio? Is it any different to other media?

In theory, radio briefs shouldn't be vastly different to the briefs you give for other media. However, as we have already seen, in reality they rarely receive the time and thought that goes into, for example, a TV brief.

Here are some key pointers for ensuring that your radio brief is both informative and inspiring for the people that will end up writing your commercials.

For reference, a recommended radio creative brief has been included at the end of this section.

First, why is radio being used?

Radio is a highly flexible medium, which means it is often asked to perform challenging tasks. It *can* carry detailed information, it *can* be booked relatively late, and it *can* be produced at short notice and at low cost, but these tend to work against high quality creativity. Advertisers have to take account of this and realise there are compromises to be made.

TIP: Be clear about the role radio is playing alongside other media in your communications plan.

Functional roles might include maintaining communication between bursts of other media; reaching people at relevant times; encouraging people to respond to other media (e.g. Internet); and communicating a variety of messages.

Emotional roles might include getting closer to consumers; becoming part of their daily lives; and speaking with them at a more human level.

Rule number one: keep it simple (no, even simpler than that!)

Advertising in any medium is always more effective when it focuses on a simple message. But with radio this is not optional, it is essential, because it's not possible to include extra information in the background or in small print.

TIP: Multiple messages? Make more commercials

As a rule of thumb, it's helpful to stick to one message per radio commercial. In this way, the writer can focus on dramatising and clarifying each individual message without having to bamboozle the listener with other confusing detail.

And as radio production is relatively cheap compared to other media, with preplanning, it's likely that recording an additional execution for your campaign will only require one extra hour in the studio plus some editing time – it is eminently affordable to produce multiple execution campaigns.

This also has the benefit of reducing the negative effects of repetition on campaign wear-out.

Beware the 'metaphorical proposition'

Radio uses words, so it invites verbal wit. If your advertising brief says something like 'our prices will take your breath away', you are likely to get creative proposals back which focus on people not breathing, holding their breath, turning purple . . . It is very rare for such ads to leave an impression about your prices. So be straightforward about your message; this will help the writers to find the best expression of it.

TIP: Ask someone to describe the ad to you

If you're not sure whether the creative device is working effectively on behalf of your brand message, ask someone to describe what happens in the commercial to you. If they can do it without mentioning your brand or offer, chances are the listener won't understand who or what it's for.

Think about 'desired response'

Don't focus the writer on what the brand is saying to the listeners. Focus instead on how we want the listeners to react. What do we want them to know, think or feel having heard the campaign? Remember, radio may only be one part of the multimedia mix, what specific response is desired for the radio component?

TIP: Be realistic in your expectations

Most advertising (unless it is offering free money) is unlikely to elicit an immediate consumer action. Generally, most advertising communication is absorbed subconsciously and helps to create or reinforce deep-seated feelings about, or attitudes towards, a brand.

In this context, it would be unrealistic for a computer company using radio to expect people to remember the specific details of memory processing speed expressed in technical language. A more realistic expectation of the listener would be that they understand this brand to be 'twice as fast', for example.

Brand tone – 'How your brand comes across'

Radio leaves strong personal impressions and it is important to recognise that all radio advertising influences the listener's impression of a brand, regardless of whether this is intended by the advertiser or not.

So, you need to clarify in the brief the kind of impression you want your brand to leave. But make sure this doesn't turn into a bland mission statement (all brands want to be seen as authoritative, contemporary and innovative).

TIP: Remember the way radio uniquely makes impressions . . .

. . . as evoked in this piece of wisdom:

'Brands are like people at parties, they make themselves look gorgeous because they want to attract your attention. With radio, your brand is addressing the blind guest at the party.'

Telephone numbers, websites, etc.

The brief needs to be clear about priorities. If the ad is thirty seconds long, do we want to spend those thirty seconds getting people to remember the telephone number or web address or getting them interested in the proposition? It's usually the latter, and consumers know how to contact most brands. The contact details are therefore relegated to being a lower priority.

TIP: Remember that radio works well as an indirect response medium

Radio has been demonstrated to be effective at driving response through other channels such as the press, door-drops or the Internet (see Section 2.4 for more details).

The briefing meeting

Once the brief is written, always try to talk it through with the writers: this will help them to understand your needs as an advertiser, and to take the brief seriously. If you invest importance in the brief, so will the people who are asked to respond to it.

TIP: Ask for the writers who are enthusiastic about radio – not all are

If the writers are radio-friendly, they're more likely to help out with potential fault lines in the brief and have a better understanding of how to find the most effective compromise between getting your message across and irritating the listener.

Radio creative brief – outline for reference
Key questions

- **What are we trying to achieve in marketing terms?**
  (e.g. gain market share through increased trial, reinforce customer loyalty, etc.).
- **What do we want the radio advertising to do within this?**
  What is the role for radio, i.e. the contribution which radio advertising can *realistically* be expected to make?
- **Who are we talking to?**
  By age/sex/class, etc., and also using vivid language. How are they related to our brand – what do they currently think/feel about us? Mention any secondary target groups, e.g. rivals, trade, etc.
- **What do we want them to think/feel/do as a result of the radio advertising campaign?**
  Realistic ambitions please; consider any secondary target audiences, e.g. those not currently in the market but may be in the future.
- **What do we want to say to them?/the proposition**
  Single-mindedness is essential here; supporting information goes below.
- **Supporting information**
  Why should they believe us or find our message relevant or interesting?
- **Tone of voice**
  How do we want to come over? Use words that describe how people relate to each other.
- **Mandatory inclusions (if any)**
  (e.g. telephone number, website, logo, etc.) Remember to keep these to a minimum.

- **Media outline**
  Which stations are we using? Are we reaching people at a particular time of day/on specific days only? What weight of activity? How many ads?

Summary – providing the optimum radio brief

- Briefing is important – if the brief is flawed, the rest of the process will struggle to overcome this.
- The most important assets that advertisers are able to add to the brief are time and thought.
- The three most important elements of the brief are:
  — identifying a proper role for radio;
  — thinking about the desired response (and being realistic);
  — nominating your desired tone of voice.
- Remember, if you as the instigator of the process take the radio brief seriously, then everyone will.

5.2 Judging good radio ideas

Judging creative proposals is an area where the advertiser can make a huge contribution – but it's not easy in any medium, and radio is no exception.

Radio ideas can be particularly hard to grasp, particularly on paper, so care must be taken to help everyone in the process understand what is being proposed.

This section offers tips and hints on judging creative proposals, with questions to ask of yourself and the writers to help you gauge whether a creative idea is promising.

It's tricky!

The issue of creativity becomes most acute for advertisers when they are required to judge creative proposals and give their approval. This is a challenging stage of the process for advertising in any medium, but perhaps even more so with radio because it is the only medium where there are no visuals to help.

The first piece of advice must be – accept that judging is difficult. This may seem counter-intuitive: radio is essentially a very simple medium, composed of words, music, sound effects and silence. But radio specialists are all agreed about this – the simplicity of radio is deceptive.

The common currency for judging radio ideas is the A4-sized script, and this is where many of the challenges originate. People imagine different things from reading the same words on paper – this is true for books and poetry as much as for radio scripts.

'When you approve a radio script, you tend to approve the words, whereas what is truly important is the effect created by the way the words work.'

Adrian Reith (creative)

'The gaps between the words are as important as the words themselves, probably more so. It's about tone.'

John Hegarty (creative)

Be clear about the role for radio

Radio is normally one part of the media mix, and is expected to do a very specific job within this. So it's important that when you are reviewing creative proposals, you narrow this down to be as focused and clear as possible.

For example, if the campaign is supposed to publicise a new addition to a range of sauces, don't expect to see all the other flavours mentioned in the ad. Radio is good at focusing on one thing. It needs to focus on one thing – there are no visuals to show all the other stuff.

In addition, always ask yourself 'How are we expecting people to respond?' Do you want people to be enthusiastic about the product offer, or remember the telephone number? If the ad tries to achieve both, it's already getting stretched.

Ask for a script to be brought to life

There are various ways to get a script brought to life, so that one can understand how it's going to work. Not all techniques suit all scripts, and circumstances vary (e.g. is there time to do a demo recording?) but here are the main techniques.

- *Getting the scripts read out.* It may seem obvious, but in fact having the scripts read out – by the writers or the agency account handler – can be a revelation. It allows your ears to process the idea, rather than your eyes (which is what happens when you read the script yourself). It's very helpful in terms of understanding the pace and tone of the commercial, and also helps to establish just how much extra room there really is in the ad: on paper it is tempting to suggest the odd additional piece of information. But when you have heard the ad take place in sound, you have a better idea of whether that additional information would over-burden it.
- *Get the ads, or demo versions, made.* The ideal solution for judging is to get the ad made and listen to it. The main downside of this is the cost – if the ad is rejected, the studio production will have to be paid for all over again. But it is worth bearing in mind that the studio production is not the

expensive part of radio advertising – the serious costs come in with actors' usage and buying airtime.

Demo tapes – rough versions of the ad – are not always useful, and opinions vary. A rough version won't help if the important point about the ad is the subtlety of its execution. This can often be true with humorous scripts – when done in rough, they may well not sound that funny.

Two techniques to help you 'get' the idea

Some radio writers recommend the use of storyboard-style presentations – graphic illustrations that depict what is happening in the ad and what should be happening in the mind's eye of the listener. This can be a very useful technique for focusing understanding of the action in a scene – for example, at www.better-radio-advertising.co.uk, listen to the ad for COI Army Recruitment (Anti-tank), and consider how a storyboard would have made clear what the listener is seeing.

Now listen to the Apple Tango ad on www.better-radio-advertising.co.uk. A storyboard presentation wouldn't have been much use. Basically, two people are having a phone conversation, and the drama lies in the edgy conflict between the characters.

The second technique is to listen to relevant audio material. In other words, if the ad is trying to create a certain kind of atmosphere, or uses a certain kind of humour, it's helpful to listen to other examples of work in the same area (this can be non-advertising audio – for example, radio drama, or comedy is a rich source of examples).

An important side-benefit of both these techniques is that they make the radio idea easier to sell on internally. If you have a boss who needs reassurance, or maybe has to approve the commercial specifically, storyboards or relevant audio examples give them something solid to hang on to while trying to assess the idea.

Casting questions

Knowing who will be acting in your commercial can be hugely helpful to understanding how it will work – with well-known actors or personalities it is often easy to imagine how the ad will sound.

However, don't be fooled by a familiar name. Not all well-known people can act, and your script may need acting skills.

'Mariella Frostrup – sexy yes, actress no. She's a presenter: you have to be aware of the difference.'

Adrian Reith (creative)

Also, consider what your well-known personality is being asked to do in the ad – will this work well in sound? We heard of an ad where the famous Formula One commentator Murray Walker was asked to sound depressed, and the result was that he became unrecognisable, since he is mainly known by his extremely enthusiastic commentary style.

The brand linkage/engagement grid

As we have already discovered, in Millward Brown's study *The Radio Awareness Multiplier*, they established that some radio campaigns can work 500 % more effectively than others, and that this was irrespective of media weight – in other words, creative content made the difference.

Their analysis concluded that the two vital dynamics for more efficient advertising were:

- ***brand linkage*** – listeners have to have a clear memory of the brand which is giving them the advertising message;
- ***engagement*** – something in the ad which makes the listener 'zone in' and pay some attention.

Using the grid in Figure 5.1, ask yourself how strongly your proposed ad is linked to the brand, and how engaging it is. With luck, your proposed ad will be in the top right-hand corner.

It's helpful to ask yourself some questions to assess the strengths of the ad.

Brand linkage
Is the ad purely relying on brand mentions to link to the brand (this is the weakest form of linkage, and quickly becomes crass

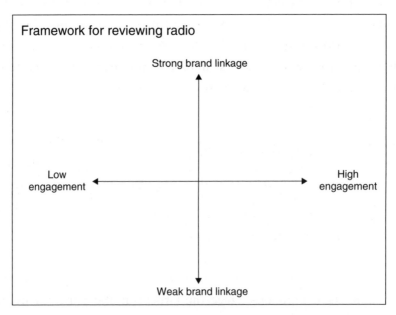

Figure 5.1 Framework for reviewing radio

and irritating); or is there something about the style or content of the ad which evokes the brand's values? Is there some sort of mnemonic, a slogan or a sonic or jingle? Some compelling radio ads leave the branding to the end (listen, for example, to Nivea for men *Parking* on www.better-radio-advertising.co.uk). For this to work well, the brand has to somehow resolve the puzzle set up by the ad, and the listener has to enjoy the ad enough to care which brand is setting up the puzzle.

Engagement

All sorts of things can make listeners zone in – curiosity, relevance, a challenge, or the familiarity of a well-known voice. There is no fixed technique to gain their attention.

Remember, ads don't have to take drastic measures to make listeners zone in – listen, for example, to Hamlet *Bummer* on www.better-radio-advertising.co.uk. This opens as a very simple, even downbeat scene where a couple are going out for the evening. Why is it so compelling? The answer is, it's a story, and human beings have a deep-seated yearning for stories – we tend to want to know what happens.

Remember too that radio ads arrive unannounced (this is very different from a TV break, where the ad break is clearly flagged, and the breaks between the ads quite often marked too). Radio listeners, therefore, just gradually find themselves listening to something that has taken their interest.

But beware the ad that tries too hard – sometimes ads use tricks to make the listener engage, and these make a negative impression (they're basically fooling people).

Essential: consider the ad's tone of voice

The truth is, it's not difficult to write a radio ad which is both memorable and well linked to the brand. However, we have all heard ads on the radio which are both unmissable and unmistakeable – and yet which are deeply irritating, all the more so when they are repeated.

So it's essential to ask yourself when judging creative work:

- What kind of impression will this advertising make?
- What tone of voice comes across?
- Does it feel right for my brand values (remember, good ads often work by changing, rather than reflecting, brand values)?

Remember, ads on radio are repeated as much as four times more often than TV ads, and over-repetition soon leads to irritation. How many ads are in your campaign, and do you need more? The answer is usually yes.

FAQ: I can remember annoying radio ads, so they obviously work don't they?

A: Any fool can get noticed on radio – it's an intrusive, real-time medium which invades people's personal space (e.g. their car) and there is very little zapping of channels (even in the car).

But the issue is *how* will your brand be noticed and remembered? Do you really want to be remembered as the crashingly predictable brand that patronises its potential customers? Not many brands can afford to be in that market position!

Specific questions to ask about dialogue ads
(based on a lecture by Mandy Wheeler)

WHO?	Who are the people in the ad? What do we know about them?
WHERE?	Where are they? What does the listener need to know about the location in order to get the point?
WHAT?	What are they talking about, and what are they saying?
WHY?	The most important question – *why* are they saying these things? What is their motivation? People need a reason to say things to other people. Once you've found the reason, the story thread comes out of this (and if there isn't a reason – 'they're just saying it' – your ad is on notice with the listener).
HOW DO I KNOW?	The listener needs to know the situation – how will this be conveyed? How will they know the location, the relationship between the characters, the action that takes place?

Three questions to ask about a proposed commercial
(based on RAB client/agency workshops)

1. What will make the listener zone in? | Why will they listen – is there a story, something which arouses curiosity? Or is it just an announcement that relies on relevance?

2. How is this linked to the brand and its message?

Make sure that the thing which makes them listen is linked securely to the brand and its message. Beware of 'disconnected' ads, where the creative bit at the start is barely linked to the product message at the end.

3. What tonal impression will the advertising leave?

What kind of tone does the advertising have? Is it what people would expect from the brand (doesn't have to be, could be a refreshing break away from the predictable). How will the brand come over, especially after the ads have been heard several times?

TIP: danger signs to watch out for on a script

Expecting too much of sound effects (SFX)
Sometimes a script will start with a sound effect which is actually a weak link, e.g. 'SFX: Sound of a balmy summer evening'. It is possible to create the sound of a balmy summer evening, but not definitively: on its own it can't set the scene. Someone in the script will have to say words which evoke the scene – then the sound effects can enhance that. Ask how the listener will understand the scene being created.

MVO, FVO
These are abbreviations for Male Voice-Over and Female Voice-Over, and used to be common shorthand in radio adver-

tising scripts. But they create problems because they do not suggest anything about the characters except their gender – this makes it difficult to understand the scene. Ask for character information about the people in the commercial.

The 'intriguing soundscape'

Radio offers an opportunity to go on a journey into sound, and inexperienced writers sometimes see this as permission to create complex and detailed soundscapes. However, they must have some dramatic content, or some framing, otherwise, the listener is inclined to zone out and think about something else. Unexplained sounds can certainly intrigue, but they can also seem irrelevant, boring or even highly irritating. Ask what will make the listener pay attention, and how they are expected to respond.

'Soundscapes or "journeys in sound" can seem attractive as ideas, but they risk being more fun to create than to listen to.'
Nick Angell

The disconnected script

Sometimes, the creativity is allowed to run away with itself a bit, and it's not unusual to hear ads where the first half is highly creative and bears little relationship to the second half, which is where the brand and message are consigned. You can sometimes spot these by the fact that the two halves are linked by a pun, or by a voice-over whose first words are 'so there you have it' (but you haven't, so they need to explain it).

An agency account handler once told us that these kinds of script are easy to sell, because the creatives and the client both like their separate bits, and the weakness of the link between them gets overlooked. Beware!

> *'Watch out for 'timeshare commercials' – this is where the agency gets the front and the client gets the back.'*
>
> Mandy Wheeler (creative)

Summary – judging good radio ideas

- Accept that judging radio is tricky: get your agency team to accept it too.
- Be very clear on the role that radio is playing: it's not good at saying two things at once.
- Beware the script on the page: ask for it to be brought to life by being read out or even recorded (but note – demo versions aren't always helpful).
- Storyboards can be helpful, as can the use of audio material from elsewhere to explain the intended tone of the ads.
- Consider all these techniques when planning how to sell the work on within your own company – what will be needed?
- Casting – be aware that famous names aren't always suitable names, so look carefully at how they fit requirements.
- The three key questions are:
  — What will make the listener zone in?
  — How is this linked to the brand and its message?
  — What tonal impression will the advertising leave?

5.3 The art of radio production

It's a bit trickier than it looks

Most people assume, very reasonably, that radio production is pretty simple, or at least straightforward. In contrast to TV advertising, which is well understood to be complex, expensive and demanding, radio is seen as quite basic – the components of voice, sound effects and music all seem familiar. There is no need for armies of technical people at the recording, and it's not a medium where fashionable new computer-generated techniques dominate executions.

It's 'only radio'. So what's so difficult about that then? Well, the reality is that it's far more complex than it looks. The bit we all understand, because we're intelligent people, is the superficial bit. Production issues here will be: who is voicing the ad? How much are they charging? Are the sound effects available (or might they need creating)? Has the music usage been agreed? Will a second voice be needed for the endline? etc.

All these are sensible questions, but they don't tell you anything about the quality of your advertising.

The advanced level issues, relating to quality, might include: have these actors worked together before (and if so, do they work well together or hate each other)? How much help will they need from a director? Will the script as written on the page deliver the atmosphere and impact we are looking for? How can we ensure the joke is truly funny in the way it comes over? What will be needed in the studio to make the ad 'work' best?

'With TV the palette is huge, with an endless range of colours and brushes available. With radio, you have only a pencil – so how you use that pencil – technique – becomes paramount.'
                                        Brian Jenkins, COI Communications

Preproduction

In TV advertising, there is always a preproduction meeting – maybe even a string of them. Everybody knows that if you don't do this, there could be some nasty surprises waiting further down the line – probably during the shoot.

People who are well-versed in the production of radio advertising advise a similar thoughtfulness with radio. Agencies will only tend to have preproduction meetings when radio commercials are particularly complex or ambitious – maybe a location recording, or several different actors, or vox pop interviews.

The reality is that preproduction can be hugely helpful for any commercial where you want a good result. It helps everyone in the process – writer, producer, director (if you are using one), account handler, client – to develop a good understanding of what is being proposed, how it is going to be executed and what will happen to make sure the best results are achieved.

It doesn't always have to be a meeting with all parties (TV pre-prods can drone on for hours). It could be a series of e-mails, or a written plan sent round to everyone. But meetings can be helpful to the process because they allow people to ask questions (even 'stupid' questions) – asking them at preproduction is so much more helpful than asking them at the studio, when the money is already being spent.

Such questions ('stupid' or otherwise) might include:

- Are we all really happy with the script – are there questions we want to ask about how it works?
- How do we expect it to change, if at all, in the studio?
- To what extent can we stray from the script if it works better?
- If the RACC have asked for terms and conditions to be added to the script, what are the implications for the rest of the commercial – will it need to be cut down? Can the conditions be included in the body of the script?
- What flexibility is there with the music? How will it be used?

The presence of a preproduction meeting forces those in the process to think through questions like these – and it is much better to tackle them at the planning stage, rather than in the studio. By the time a script gets to the studio, the actors will want to be confident that everyone knows what is required, and the studio will want to know how long the session is. Over-runs are possible, and some people even rely on them, but they sap the enthusiasm of actors, producers, engineers and directors, and should be avoided. The same goes for re-recordings. Good planning obviates any need for them, and saves money.

Casting

We have already seen in Section 5.2 on approving creative proposals, that casting needs an experienced hand, and clarity about what is required from the voice actor.

A first issue to be aware of is that there are broadly three kinds of voice to choose from:

1. **Actors/voice actors** – these are people who act (and who usually act in TV or theatre as well as radio), and can therefore use their acting skills to create atmosphere, bring meaning, find the subtext in a piece of writing and perhaps use improvisation skills to develop the scripts. These skills are not much to do with quality of voice, and everything to do with acting ability.

2. **Voice-overs** – these are people who are typically employed to voice slogans, endlines or announcements. The quality of their voice is what tends to get them work. They are not actors, although sometimes they are asked to act – when this happens, the results can sound underwhelming or amateurish.

3. **Personalities** – these are people who are asked to appear in radio ads because of who they are. When listeners recognise

them (and sometimes listeners will need to be told who they are), this can bring status or excitement to a commercial. They are usually asked to be themselves, as this is what gets them recognised – beware however, if they are asked to speak or behave differently from their known traits. People in this category may or may not be able to act: it depends on their background and experience.

This is not an official categorisation of the voice talent available, but it describes the main groupings. There are overlaps of course. The point is, you need to be clear what kind of voice talent your commercial needs – does it need acting skills? Or would a voice-over be sufficient?

Exercise: Listen to Wella Shock Waves *Toilet* on www.better-radio-advertising.co.uk. The voice of Vic Reeves has clearly been used for the effect his personality brings. But what about the character of the father – would you want a voice-over, or an actor?

Who's directing?

An increasing number of agencies now use directors for their radio advertising – over two-thirds of the finalists in the 2004 Aerial Awards used a director.

As a client you may wonder what the point of a radio director is: without this understanding, their presence may just look like an expensive addition to the production costs of your campaign.

Our experience suggests that, although they are not always necessary in the process, there are many benefits to involving directors.

The independent advisor

Agencies and clients sometimes get into wrangles about what will work in the commercial; it can be helpful to have an impartial director in the process to offer advice about what would deliver the best result.

Better communication in the studio

Figures 5.2 and 5.3 were created by radio commercials director Martin Sims. In Figure 5.2, everybody is talking to everybody in the studio, and the result is that the actor becomes confused

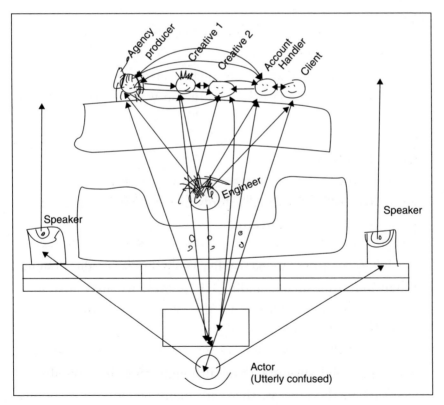

Figure 5.2 Studio protocol 1: how not to do it

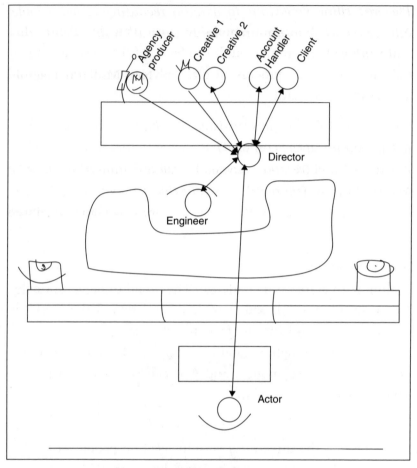

Figure 5.3 Studio protocol 2: why a director helps

about the advice he/she is being given. The actor ends up speaking back to the whole room via the speakers, which creates more problems.

By contrast, in Figure 5.3, the director becomes the central point for all the participants, so the actor gets notes from only one person, and speaks to that person with any questions or suggestions.

'The last thing you want in a radio recording is five people telling you what to do – inevitably they all want slightly different things.'

Neil Mullarkey (actor)

'Muhammad Ali always insisted on having just one voice talking to him in the corner. That's what actors want. It's what they get in theatre and television – there is one director, and everyone knows you have to turn to that person.'

Simon Greenall (actor)

Dealing with actors

Dealing with actors is a challenge. They tend to be neurotic (by their own admission), and they don't understand the world of advertising. Add to this the fact that they are put into a small booth with a microphone and have six people staring at them while they talk for money, and you can understand why it's rather pressurising for them.

So the task of the director is very focused on people skills. He has to get the actors to get comfortable with the script, feel that they can contribute, feel valued in the process, and give their best performance. Alongside this, he also has to ask them to do it maybe eight times, maybe twenty-eight times, and each time he has to find a way to make them do it which takes the production another step towards the best possible result.

These issues are multiplied many times over if you are working with two or more actors at the same time.

Some creatives direct their own radio commercials, but the ones who are good at it tend to have good people skills.

Allowing for development in the studio

If you don't have any experience of radio production, you tend to believe that the words on the page are going to be the words in the commercial. In fact, a comparison of ads with their originals always reveals that something changes during studio production. It may be a couple of words or a phrase. It can sometimes be a whole tranche of the script, with a new character being introduced, or perhaps the characters swapping the lines they say.

The reality is that actors often find, when they are working up the script in the studio, that little changes work really well: they improve the tone and mood of a script, and add impact and humour. It's very difficult to predict before the studio session how these improvements will unfold – you just have to try them out and see what works well.

'Radio is a creative process, and the actors are one of the most creative parts. You have to allow them to bring their creativity to the script: it's invaluable.'

Clive Brill (radio drama producer)

An example we heard of was where a script originally had the actor saying 'What? You must be out of your . . .', but in the studio, the actor found it was much funnier if he left a pause and said 'Helloooo?' A different actor might not have had the same experience.

It is vital for you as a client to acknowledge that these in-studio changes can be important and helpful, and to give enough permission for them to happen. Try not to get yourself into the situation where every word of a script has been signed off and is immutable.

Summary – the art of radio production

- Accept that production is tricky: ask your agency to take it seriously, ask for the people who are good at radio.
- Preproduction helps: it's essential to get buy-in and clarity about issues like sound effects, music and tone before the studio session, not during it.
- In casting, consider the type of performer: beware of the differences between voice actors, voice-overs and personalities – select on the basis of the skills they bring.
- Understand the value that radio directors can add: their expertise and impartiality could be what you need to get the best result.
- Actors need good direction: if your agency has no experienced directors, consider using an external radio director.
- Allow room for development in the studio: as the client, you can create permission for the final touches of magic which happen in the studio.

5.4 Branding in sound

'I cannot think of a single reason why any radio advertiser would not want to use some kind of sonic branding. Would any advertiser ever put out a press ad that didn't bear a logo?'

Dan Jackson (author of *Sonic Branding*)

It's hard to disagree with Dan's sentiment, yet still the majority of radio commercials rarely feature any form of consistent branding. So why is the use of audio branding so limited?

First, we have to look back at the development of modern marketing communications. The visual media of posters, press and packaging dominated the early years of brand marketing and necessarily led to a reliance on visual branding properties. As a result, many marketing companies have visual brand guidelines that date back decades, based on original packaging brand properties developed around the beginning of the 20th century (e.g. Marmite).

At 30 years old, commercial radio in the UK is a relative newcomer to the media family and the only one that necessitates some form of audio branding, because visual brand properties are rendered useless. Radio's 'outsider' status was compounded by the medium's inability to shake off its '2 % medium' tag for the first twenty years of its life, meaning that the advertising world had a ready excuse to ignore audio branding.

The dominance of visual brand identities over audio is highlighted in research amongst delegates at the 2004 RAB Advertiser Conference, with 89 % claiming to have visual brand guidelines and only 29 % with sonic brand guidelines (Figure 5.4). Even these figures are likely to be inflated by the fact that the majority of respondents were existing radio advertisers.

However, interest in sonic branding is growing, possibly attributable to the increasing importance of media neutral thinking in developing communication ideas – in this context, all brand touch points offer the opportunity to positively influence the consumer's impression of a brand. When the list of touch points is extended to include call centres, retail environments, events, websites and office spaces, in addition to TV commercials and other audio-visual opportunities, it is easy to understand why

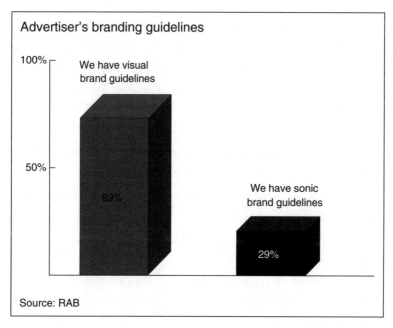

Figure 5.4 The dominance of visual branding vs. audio

brand owners are keen to benefit from the incremental branding opportunities that can be unlocked by sound.

How does sonic branding work?

The brain processes memory and music in the same way; in this way, words attached to music can be learnt more quickly and retained for longer. This applies as much to advertising messages as it does to popular music. So, by using music as a consistent part of brand expression, a brand's advertising can be made more effective.

The following is an extract from an article about how music can help people learn and retain advertising messages written by Dan Jackson in *FT Creative Business* on 28th September 2004:

There are three categories of sound we can hear: voice, ambience and music. Each enters the ear as vibrations and is converted into a code of neuro-signals. There is no sound in your brain, only electricity. How the brain processes each category is different:

- *words are processed in the left hemisphere, though the rhythms of speech patterns are right brain;*
- *ambient sounds are the product of spatial awareness and are mainly right brain;*
- *music lights up the whole brain like Blackpool Beach during a power-surge; tempo on the left, melody and harmony on the right, advanced emotional meaning in the pre-frontal cortex, basic emotions in the low-down amygdala.*

The only thing that lights up the brain in the same way as music is memory. Both of these share neural pathways throughout the brain. This is what makes music so memorable and what makes memories so easy to conjure up through music.

Consider how much music you know and how it can change how you feel; bringing back memories of a school disco slow dance, a holiday, being dumped, getting married or any of the countless times in life where music has accompanied an event or happening.

Musical messages, together with memories, need to be consistently reinforced, heard and processed with regularity, for them to become enduring neural pathways in the brain. Herein lies the marketing opportunity and the essence of what is termed sonic branding.

> *If a brand uses music consistently across time and touch point to accompany its marketing messages (and by consistently, I mean broadly the same piece of music every time), then a lasting emotional memory of those communications will form in the listener. This will outlast any other marketing communication. Think back to the musical ads of your youth and how their place in your memory endures. At the most basic level, think Shake 'n' Vac.*
>
> *Brands that invest in consistent sounds find a path directly to the hearts and minds of consumers.*

The business case for developing sonic branding

So, brain science demonstrates that linking a branded message with a consistent piece of music can enhance the effectiveness of communication. This is true at a media neutral level, not just for radio. However, let's consider the specific benefits of sonic branding for the radio advertiser:

- *It provides unmistakable branding.* Consumers famously don't care which brand an advertisement is for – sonic branding implicitly (and subconsciously) confirms the identity of the brand.
- *It goes in 'under the radar'.* It allows an advertiser to deliver a branded 30-second message without requiring the attention of the listener; sonic branding is recalled easily, even by those listening who felt they were paying little or no attention.
- *It can help develop favourable brand perceptions.* Most sonic branding is musical and evocative rather than verbal and hard-sell; this allows it to be repeated continually, gradually adapting the consumer's brand perceptions.

- *It increases radio advertising effectiveness.* In the Millward Brown *Awareness Multiplier* study (see Chapter 4 and Section 5.2) we learnt how the most effective ads were both engaging and were strongly linked to the brand. These factors contributed to a difference in effectiveness of up to 500 %. It seems reasonable therefore that an advertiser with an established piece of sonic branding will automatically benefit from radio advertising of above average effectiveness.

Which brands can benefit most?

It is clear that sonic branding can have a significant business effect. But what sort of brands stand to gain the most from developing their own sonic branding? Here are our views on the categories that can benefit most.

Brands under pressure from competitive noise

Using sonic branding ensures that every advertising message is effectively branded, thus maximising branded presence in the mind of the consumer.

Example: British Airways have used the same sonic identity (Flower Duet from *Lakme* by Delibes) for almost 20 years. This piece of music (which helps conjure up images of soaring above the clouds) is featured on all of their advertising, through to their telephone hold system, in the shuttles at Gatwick and onboard the aircraft prior to take-off. The consistency and longevity of usage mean that their advertising is instantly recognisable as BA, even when the music is played at a different tempo with unusual instruments (featured on www.better-radio-advertising.co.uk).

Brands with little 'news' for consumers

There are many brands, typically in the fmcg area, where the brand name and proposition are widely known, but there is nothing genuinely new to say about the brand. In cases like these, sounds and music can create high levels of awareness with a generic message.

Example: As a cigar brand, there was very little news for Hamlet to tell consumers about. Yet for over 30 years they remained one of the most high profile advertised brands in the UK, even when regulation meant that they were no longer able to advertise on TV and advertised on radio alone. A major factor in this success was the consistent use of Bach's *Air on a G string* as a sonic branding device. It has been suggested that the effectiveness of the sonic branding was enhanced by the way in which it was used to 'resolve' the dramatic tension developed in each commercial.

Brands of 'low interest' or with a long purchase cycle

In low interest categories, such as technology or personal finance, the consumer tends to resist the overtures of advertisers seeking his attention, until such time as he is actively in the market. Using sonic branding allows basic branded communication without requiring the explicit attention of the consumer – by the time the consumer comes in to the market, the sonic branding has built a large advance share of mind.

Example: An extremely important element of the way radio built the Carphone Warehouse brand was the consistent use of music (principally the *Connected* theme by the Stereo MCs) to ensure that people registered a brand message even if they were not ready to listen to information about telephony. This ability of sonic branding to go in 'under the radar' has been one of the most conspicuously effective aspects of the brand's advertising history.

Developing a sonic brand identity

When advertisers challenge their agencies about how their radio advertising will be distinctively recognisable as coming from their brand, a common response is 'we'll develop a sonic mnemonic in the studio'. This type of approach belittles the strength of sonic branding and relegates it to just an executional device. And it rarely reaps any benefits as the resulting sound is employed only in the radio advertising and has little or no strategic link to the brand.

Developing effective sonic branding, like developing visual branding, is a specialist area that consists of a process that requires considerable investment of time and thought (and money). To be truly successful, the results of the process should be employed in an appropriate manner across all brand touch points.

There are now specialist companies, such as *sonicbrandcompany* and *SonicSista*, springing up to meet the demands of brands keen to benefit from sonic brand properties, each of which has its own unique development processes.

If you're considering developing your own sonic branding property, here are our top five tips, based on our observations of the more successful proponents.

TIP 1: Plan in advance and consult the experts

If you're planning to develop sonic branding guidelines for your brand, don't leave it to the engineer to come up with something when he's recording your radio commercial. Plan in advance and consult the experts to help diagnose the most powerful means of expressing your brand in sound across all of its touch points.

TIP 2: Be clear about the requirements

What does the sonic branding need to do in the marketing mix? Does it have to build the personality of the brand, or just be consonant with it? Does it have to build familiarity or actually change perceptions of the brand? Generally speaking, the simpler the requirements of the sonic branding property, the more effective it will be.

TIP 3: Make it unmistakable

The ultimate goal is for sonic branding which cannot be recalled without thinking of the brand in question.

TIP 4: Make sure it works in the long term

It takes time for sonic branding to become truly linked to the brand. This is particularly true where the sonic is a borrowed property (e.g. an existing song). The long-term requirement also means that your sonic branding must be pleasant enough and adaptable enough to work consistently over time.

TIP 5: Establish the property across all touch points

This is a strategy adopted by many advertisers and exemplifies the point that there has to be an initial 'investment phase' during which the sonic brand property is established. In this context, it is worth remembering that the strongest and longest-lasting sonic brand properties from the past were created on the back of TV campaign weights that these days would be unaffordable – so there is a sound business case for media-neutral sonic brand properties.

5.5 Summary – branding in sound

- Branding in sound is not just beneficial to radio advertisers (although it does provide them with a distinct advantage), yet few brands have exploited it to the same degree as visual branding.
- There is a business case for investing in sonic branding, as when used optimally it can help consumers learn commercial messages more quickly and retain them for longer.
- Sonic branding is particularly beneficial for brands that are under pressure from competitive media noise; brands with little 'news' for consumers; and 'low interest' brands/brands with a long purchase cycle.
- If developing sonic branding, it is important to treat the process seriously, as when developing visual brand guidelines s– specialist companies exist in this field.
- To establish a sonic branding property as quickly and effectively as possible, it should be used across all brand touch points. Sonic branding that is isolated in radio advertising, which in turn forms part of a multimedia schedule, is rarely successful.

6
Measuring Radio's Effect

Many advertisers have to learn the hard way – don't be one of them!

The effect of radio is a little bit tricky to measure (this seems to be related to the conversational or 'unofficial' way it communicates with the listener – people may have got the message, they just can't remember where from).

There are some easy tips and techniques here to help you overcome these pitfalls – particularly using split samples in any research (listeners and non-listeners).

This section gives advice all the way through the process – from setting research objectives through to reading the results.

6.1 Defining the research objectives

The key to any successful research is to have a clear understanding of why the research is being conducted in the first place. In other words, what are you aiming to measure?

In broad terms, radio advertising research aims can be categorised into two types:

- *Marketing issues* – to what extent has radio helped to achieve the campaign aims?
- *Media planning issues* – what effect do different media strategies have on the performance of the campaign?

Marketing issues

These vary widely and there can often be more than one objective set for a campaign. Below are some typical examples:

- increase sales;
- increase footfall/store traffic;
- increase brand awareness;
- change consumers' perceptions about a brand;
- broaden consumer appeal.

Not all of these aims are best evaluated with consumer survey research – there are specific tools available for measuring sales effects, for example.

Media planning issues

In addition to tracking radio's contribution to the success of a campaign, as a secondary aim you might also be trying to test and evaluate the effects of using different media strategies, for example:

- the effectiveness of different spot lengths;
- burst versus continuous activity;
- the use of different day part strategies.

If you do intend to test a particular media strategy, there are three important considerations to note.

1. Most obviously, you must gear the campaign so that you can test the particular media strategy in which you are interested.
2. If you are testing a number of media strategies simultaneously, you will need to be able to separate the effects of each using a separate, balanced research 'cell' for each media variable.
3. When testing different media strategies, bear in mind that you will still be judging the effects in terms of the overall campaign objectives.

Whatever your research objectives, once you have defined them, make sure that they form the core of the questionnaire you use. Any other questions are of secondary importance.

TIP: Setting realistic objectives

Researchers and planners agree it is extremely difficult to change perceptions of a brand over a short period unless there is something particular and engaging to tell the consumer.

Most advertising campaigns are tasked with increasing or maintaining awareness of brands which are already familiar to the consumer – and therefore have slower-to-change perceptions.

6.2 The importance of split samples

Misattribution of advertising

When asked to consider advertising, consumers will turn their thoughts to the most salient source they can think of – this tends to mean TV. Television tends to dominate memories of advertising, with the result that campaigns in all other media are, to varying extents, attributed to television in the consumer's mind.

This misattribution is disproportionately likely to happen with radio and is still more likely to happen when radio campaigns are creatively synergistic with TV executions.

Avoiding misattribution by using split samples

The simplest solution to the problem of measuring true radio awareness is to split your sample into two parts: listeners (target consumers who have been listening to the radio stations which carried the advertising) and non-listeners (people who do not listen to those stations, but who are the same as the listeners in all other respects).

If the only difference between the two samples is their radio listening, then any differences in their awareness or attitudes to the advertised brand can be reasonably attributed to radio – regardless of where they think they have seen or heard the advertising.

It is particularly important to use split samples where radio is part of a mixed media schedule, in order to gauge the true radio effect.

6.3 Where to do the research

Test and control samples in different areas

This involves taking two matched samples of respondents in different geographical areas and comparing their advertising responses – one sample will live in the advertised area, the other in an area where no radio advertising ran.

In this way, it will be possible to compare the results among those who have been exposed to the campaign with the results among those who have not – thus giving you a measure of radio's effectiveness (Figure 6.1).

It is important to match the media consumption of the samples (e.g. how much TV they watch, etc.) as well as their demographics, as this could affect response. It is equally important to

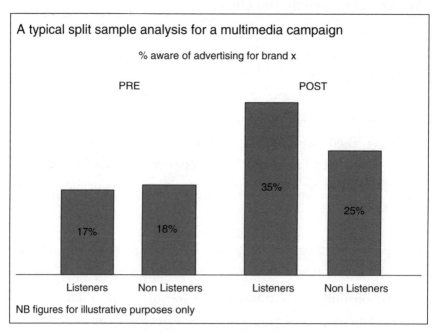

Figure 6.1 A typical split sample analysis for a multimedia campaign

ensure weight of advertising for your brand in all other media is the same for both samples.

The two geographical areas should also be comparable (or 'typical') in terms of media and product consumption as a whole.

Test and control samples within the same area

In this second approach, all of the research is done within the same area. One part of the sample will comprise people who do listen to the station(s) on your radio schedule, whilst the other part of the sample will comprise people who do not listen to any station on your schedule.

Again, in this way it will be possible to compare the results of those who have been exposed to the campaign to those who have not, giving you a measure of radio's effectiveness.

Which option should you choose?

Neither of the two approaches above is necessarily better than the other. You might want to bear in mind, however, that the second method has the advantage of questioning people who will have the same history of exposure to your brand. Local distribution levels for the brand will also be the same.

But remember that for some target markets, such as young people, it can be hard to recruit a sample of non-listeners in the same area (sometimes almost all of them listen to commercial radio).

The key point is that the listener and non-listener samples must be matched as closely as possible in terms of demographics, media consumption and weight of exposure to your advertising in other media. This ensures that any differences can confidently be attributed to radio ad exposure.

TIP: Heavy, medium and light listeners

Asking listeners how many hours a day they listen to a given station allows you to categorise them by weight of listening – this can be broken out on the analysis.

This can be useful. For example, if increased response is positive but actually confined to heavy listeners, there may well be a mandate for increasing frequency against medium and light listeners.

6.4 When to do the research

The ideal research method is to monitor advertising activity on a continuous basis, since this allows movements in advertising response to be compared directly to current advertising activity. Often, however, continuous radio research is impractical on grounds of cost, unless it forms part of ongoing advertising tracking.

Typically, radio research is conducted in two stages – a pre-campaign and a post-campaign study.

- The **pre-campaign** study should be conducted as close to the start of the radio campaign as possible – preferably during the week immediately preceding the radio campaign. This will establish the base levels of whatever is being measured (e.g. brand awareness).
- The **post campaign** study should be conducted as soon as possible after the radio campaign has ended – ideally during the first week after the campaign has come off air.

In some instances you might want to consider conducting more than two stages of research. For example, it might be worth slotting in an additional research phase during a particularly long advertising campaign or sponsorship. Similarly, having done the post research, you might want to consider adding an additional stage of research some weeks after a campaign has ended in order, say, to track decay in brand awareness.

TIP: No time for a pre-stage measure?

There is a 'rough and ready' solution for times when a pre-stage has not been possible.

If non-listeners are used as a control sample (i.e. people who would not have been exposed to the radio advertising campaign) they are, in a sense, equivalent to a pre-stage sample.

In other words, the difference, following a radio campaign, between a matched sample of listeners and non-listeners, is equivalent to the difference between listeners before and after a campaign. If you need to consider this as an option, remember the following:

- it does not take account of your other media activity;
- it does not take account of anything else which happened during the radio campaign (e.g. competitive activity, etc.).

6.5 Sample sizes

Generally speaking, the larger the sample the better. However, at some point, the cost of an increased sample size becomes cost prohibitive and contributes little extra to statistical robustness.

	Minimum sample size	Suggested sample size
Pre-research		
Listeners/test sample	200	400
Non-listeners/control sample	200	400
	400	**800**
Post-campaign		
Listeners/test sample	200	400
Non-listeners/control sample	200	400
	400	**800**
Total	**800**	**1600**

Figure 6.2 Minimum and suggested sample sizes

Figure 6.2 shows details of what would often be recommended as minimum and suggested sample sizes. Note, however, that if you intend to analyse the results amongst subgroups of your target audience, a larger sample will probably be required. As a general rule, the greater the complexity of the task, the larger the sample size needed. Your research agency can advise on this.

TIP: The advertising target audience defines the sample

If the advertising is tasked with changing the attitudes of ABC1s, is there any reason to gauge the views of C2DEs?

6.6 Method and questionnaire

Telephone research is often used for assessing the effect of radio campaigns: the method is adaptable and can often be cheaper than face-to-face interviewing. Radio ads can successfully be played down the phone to respondents.

Face-to-face interviewing may be preferable if respondents need to be shown visual ad material, such as stills from TV ads.

Commercial recognition is a valuable technique – i.e. playing the radio ads to consumers – as this is the best 'memory jogger' of all. It also delivers a larger sample of people who are identifiable as having definitely heard the campaign: this is useful when analysing them for their attitudes to the brand.

Note that when playing radio commercials in order to measure commercial recognition, two different approaches can be taken: blind or branded.

- *Blind.* By bleeping out all brand references in each execution and asking whether the commercial has been heard before, and then asking for the brand name, it is possible to see whether creative treatment has successfully linked the message to the brand.
- *Branded.* This allows prompting for brand-specific data (e.g. attitudes to the advertising/feelings about the proposition), whilst giving a true measure of ad recognition.

A fairly straightforward questionnaire will take around 10–15 minutes to run through – much longer and respondents will begin to lose interest and concentration!

Questionnaire structure

It is important to ensure your research agency's draft questionnaire includes all your original aims to ensure survey results
encompass all factors you wanted to measure.

Pre- and post-campaign questionnaires will largely be the same
(although the former can often be shorter).

Key elements of a typical pre- and post-campaign research study
are detailed below.

Typical elements of pre- and post-research questionnaires

- General questions on the category in which your brand
  operates
- General questions on brand usage and advertising awareness
- General questions on media consumption, and specifically
  questions that can separate listeners to the radio stations
  used in the campaign from non-listeners
- Recall of advertising. At the post-stage, you will be seeking
  to detect spontaneous and prompted awareness
- Commercial recognition – playing the ads to respondents
- Thoughts on what the main message of the ads was

6.7 Measuring the short-term sales effects of radio

Any advertiser that has access to sales data for their product by
postal sector is able to measure the sales uplift of a specific radio
campaign, providing that suitable test and control regions are
identified (see Section 6.3).

To calculate the uplift in sales attributable to radio, the differences in customer spend between the test and control regions in

the period before radio advertising takes place need to be identified. This provides information about the differences in purchasing habits between the two customer groups during a period of no radio advertising.

This difference can then be used to calculate an expected customer spend in the test region based on changes in sales in the control region across the period when the radio advertising is active.

The difference between this expected customer spend and the actual spend in the test region identifies the uplift that can be solely attributed to the effect of radio advertising, as this is the only variable between the two regions.

The use of existing sales data, coupled with the test and control methodology, effectively negates the need for an expensive tracking sample. As a result, the overall costs involved in sales effects research tend to be lower than those associated with traditional media tracking research, and are a small fraction of the average campaign cost.

Depending upon the detail of the sales data available, it may also be possible to track the longer-term behaviour of consumers who come into a brand because of the radio advertising. Not only can this provide an insight into the cumulative effect of repeat advertising on the loyalty of these consumers, it can also provide valuable information on the long-term value of advertising.

6.8 Measuring the effect of radio sponsorships and promotions

The same rules apply to measuring radio; however, there are some additional aspects that are particularly important to bear in mind when considering measuring radio S&P.

As ever, the first rule is to be clear on what you are measuring.

What are the main communication objectives?

Research objectives should always match advertising/marketing objectives, this is equally true of S&P. Think about the purpose behind the sponsorship or promotion – what are you trying to achieve? What role is it playing within your overall media mix?

For example:

- increase awareness/extend brand presence;
- reinforce brand values/change perceptions;
- generate response/website registrations.

If you are using a short-term promotion to drive direct response/ website registrations, it's possible to just measure these in isolation. More complex brand communication objectives (building awareness, changing perceptions, etc.) require consumer research.

How well are the executional elements working?

S&P offers brands the opportunity to benefit from association with a particular programme or presenter. However, listener research suggests that the way this association is implemented is crucial to its success, so you should always consider measuring the executional elements to understand how these have contributed to the overall effect of the association.

Consider prompting listeners with sponsor credits/live reads/ trails and getting their reactions to them in order to understand how well the mechanics are working from a listener perspective, i.e. are they helping or hindering the overall brand communication?

Be clear about who you want to measure

It is important to measure the correct audience that your S&P activity is aimed at (this could be a subaudience within your overall brand communication objectives). If a particular station has been chosen to communicate highly targeted messages, then only measure listeners to that station. This is particularly crucial where a station's output has a very strong brand identity and exclusive audience profile, e.g. XFM.

By researching listeners to your S&P host station you will obtain more realistic measures about how people feel about the brand and execution (in contrast, someone who doesn't listen to XFM because they don't particularly like its format is unlikely to respond favourably to a promotion which has been exclusively developed to suit the XFM audience).

The relevance of split samples

We have already covered the benefits of split sample methodology for measuring radio advertising activity, and it is equally relevant for measuring the effects of radio sponsorships and promotions.

Ideally, you should measure any key changes in awareness/perceptions (or other specific S&P campaign objectives) amongst listeners to the radio station that is 'hosting' the S&P property, and compare these to people who don't listen to the station. However, it is very important to ensure that your listener/non-listener samples are equally matched in terms of demographics, media consumption and exposure to all other advertising/marketing activity for the brand.

Where S&P is used alongside spot advertising on radio, the only way to identify the incremental impact of the S&P element in terms of brand awareness/perceptions would be to introduce a further control sample of people exposed to the advertising but not the S&P.

When to do the research

As with measurement of any radio campaign, ideally carry out a pre-test just before the start of the S&P activity and then post-test immediately afterwards. If any build-up to the promotion has been planned (e.g. prerecorded trails, DJ mentions), make sure the pre-test is carried out just before this, otherwise your pre-dip will already be in the early stages of being influenced by the promotion.

For longer-term sponsorship activity, it may be worth thinking about additional dips during the activity, budget permitting.

6.9 Summary

- Radio effectiveness research requires clarity of objectives – what are the agreed objectives of the overall campaign and of the radio campaign within this? Remember not all objectives can best be measured by consumer research (e.g. sales effects).
- Radio effectiveness can be measured either using continuous research or in stages ('pre and post') the pre-stage is normally

the week before the campaign, the post-stage in the week after the campaign finishes.

- Consumers tend to misattribute radio advertising memories to other media, particularly TV. This is particularly likely to happen where there is a strong executional link between the two media and/or where there is an established history of TV advertising for the brand.

- This tendency to misattribute can be offset by using matched samples of listeners and non-listeners. This way, if the increase in advertising awareness is greater among listeners than it is among non-listeners, then the effect can be attributed to radio fairly confidently – even if the listeners think the advertising was in another medium.

- Radio research can successfully be done using telephone interviewing – ads can be played down the line. However, in cases where other media are to be included in the research, it might be more appropriate to use face-to-face interviewing.

- Commercial recognition is a valuable technique – i.e. playing the ads to consumers. It provides a more robust measure of whether they have heard the campaign, and avoids problems of trying to describe the ads. Brand names can be bleeped out of the commercial to test whether the campaign is linked to the brand.

- It is possible to measure the short-term sales effects of radio using test and control region methodology.

- Measuring radio sponsorships and promotions is also possible but requires special consideration and careful planning.

SECTION 3
THINKING ABOUT
RADIO AS
'NEW MEDIA'

In this section we explore the societal trends that are changing consumer behaviour towards brands. We consider how marketing, and radio advertising in particular, can develop to meet the challenges that this presents, and offer examples of advertisers who have already explored this territory.

Chapter 7   The New Challenges Facing Brand Communications

- The evolving consumer context
- How brand marketing is changing
- Dialogue, the new brand driver
- Summary

Chapter 8   Radio's Role in Emerging Brand Thinking

- Radio as a brand conversation medium
- Harnessing the power of radio for brand conversations
- New conversational roles for radio
- Summary

7

The New Challenges Facing Brand Communications

Advertising is changing. It is being obliged to do so by changes in society and in the relationships that people have with brands – the old model of advertising is no longer the panacea it seemed to be.

On the one hand, this means pressure – brands that do not adapt will be under threat. On the other hand, brands that learn new ways to communicate can look forward to an enriched interaction with consumers.

In this chapter we look at these changes and the factors behind them – and the way in which dialogue (or conversation) between brands and consumers promises to be a core component of future marketing.

7.1 The evolving consumer context

There are two main drivers that are responsible for the way consumer behaviour relating to brands is evolving:

- declining trust in traditional institutions;
- the rise of technology/accessibility of information.

Declining trust

Recent Henley Centre research, illustrated in Figure 7.1, highlighted the declining levels of public confidence and trust in traditional sources of authority, such as the State, the Church or the legal system (e.g. in 2000, only 15 % of people trusted Parliament to be honest and fair, compared with 54 % in 1983).

Hand in hand with this trend, the rolling back of the State has encouraged or forced consumers to take personal responsibility for many 'life management' decisions previously made on their behalf by institutions.

However, this 'liberation' in terms of consumer choice is also enslaving due to the sheer volume of options available, coupled with the lack of expertise to choose between them and the potentially high penalties of making the wrong decision.

During the 1990s, it seemed that commercial brands were ideally positioned to fill the 'trust vacuum' created in the wake of institutional decline, by promising consistent quality of product and service and helping consumers to make choices.

However, during the last few years, The Henley Centre's research has demonstrated that trust in brands is also becoming more conditional – consumers now require their trust to be

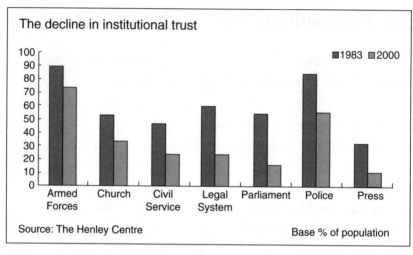

Figure 7.1 The decline in institutional trust

properly earned and continually re-earned – blind faith is no longer proffered in any sphere of their lives.

Faced with a far greater availability in choice and declining trust in the traditional methods of navigating this choice, how are consumers informing the decision-making process nowadays?

The rise of technology and 'Informationalism'

In recent years there has been rapid take-up of digital technology (Figure 7.2). Demand seems to constantly accelerate to meet the increasing supply of new devices. This is particularly evident in the wealth of new technology relating to better and more readily available access to information via the Internet, such as broadband, wireless laptops, Internet-enabled mobile phones and PDAs.

The sociologist Manuel Castells identified the effects of the rise of the Internet, which he described as 'Informationalism', a tech-

Increased take-up and use of technology		
	2003	2007
% Adults 15+ using Internet	50	56
% Households with digital TV	50	80
% Households with broadband	7	19
Source: Future Foundation, Interactive Advertising Bureau (NOP)		

Figure 7.2 Increased take-up and use of technology

nology driven change in the organisation of society, in his study of *The Rise of the Network Society.*

Brand consultant John Grant developed this theme in his book *After Image* by highlighting how Informationalism has huge implications for society at all levels: economics, markets, companies and individuals: 'It has revolutionised the capital markets and nation state politics. It also changes people's minds.'

Focusing on the last of these, it is generally accepted that information technology empowers people (Castells noted that the Internet was technology for 'self-reinforcing, accelerated learning'). Greater access to information means that it is easier than ever for people to develop their own opinions on even the most specialist topics by accumulating personal knowledge and understanding of them. This can happen almost instantly, as and when the knowledge is required. John Grant calls this 'learning just-in-time'.

In many markets, especially high-ticket or high-interest markets, the Internet is often used as a research tool as well as a channel for buying (Figure 7.3). Consumers are consequently better informed about a brand/product from a variety of sources, including current or competitive users, as opposed to the sole

What people use the Internet for	
Research	92%
Communication with friends	88%
Product information	73%
Hobby information	70%
News	70%
Instant messages	56%
Entertainment	50%
Communication	48%
Source: Connectis supplement, Financial Times May 2001	

Figure 7.3 Percentage of Internet users using it regularly for the above activities

perspective of the company that owns the brand. This in turn helps them to make more active decisions about the brands they choose.

7.2 How brand marketing is changing

'Prosumers' and the declining power of image advertising

We've seen in the last section how a combination of declining trust and accessibility of information is enabling consumers to make more active and better-informed choices about brands. The American futurist Alvin Toffler coined an expression to reflect this new model of consumer influence: 'the prosumer'.

'As prosumers we have a new set of responsibilities to educate ourselves. We are no longer a passive market upon which industry dumps consumer goods, but a part of the process, pulling toward us the information and services that we design from our own imagination.'

Alvin Toffler

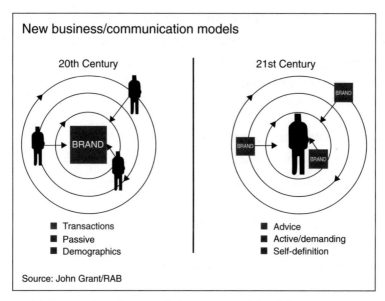

Figure 7.4 Twentieth and twenty-first century models of the brand – consumer relationship

The prosumer concept challenges the late 20th century model of the brand–consumer relationship. In this, the brand is considered to be at the centre of the universe with passive consumers orbiting it, being pulled towards it through the gravitational strength of its aspirational brand image (see the left-hand side of Figure 7.4).

Increasingly, companies are realising that individual consumers actually occupy the centre, with the brands orbiting them (see the right-hand side of Figure 7.4). The consumers are best-placed (and better-informed) to make the brand choices that most suit their individual requirements.

In this new model, it is the company that best understands and connects with the individual that will be rewarded with their custom.

In this redefined relationship between brands and consumer, the customer is better informed and more in control, and the dominance of traditional brand-image advertising in influencing consumer opinion is reduced.

The new marketing approach

So, how can brands connect with consumers better in this new model of the marketing universe?

In his book *The New Marketing Manifesto*, John Grant explores some key principles to help encourage consumers to engage with brands and pull them into their world:

- be *intimate* – get as close as possible to people's lives;
- be *relevant* – tap into the needs, changing lives and mentality of your audience;
- be *participative* – allow the active and media-literate audience to get involved in interesting ways;
- be *consensual* – put the audience at the centre of your activities and make word of mouth your main medium.

Overall, these principles reflect a need to involve people in brand ideas that are relevant in their lives – a clear step forward from the traditionally one-dimensional approach of most image-based advertising.

7.3 Dialogue, the new brand driver

Evolution in communication technology has seen a global surge in dialogue in recent years, driven by consumers adapting new technology (camera-enabled mobile phones, e-mail, text messaging) to act as an intermediate means of conversation when

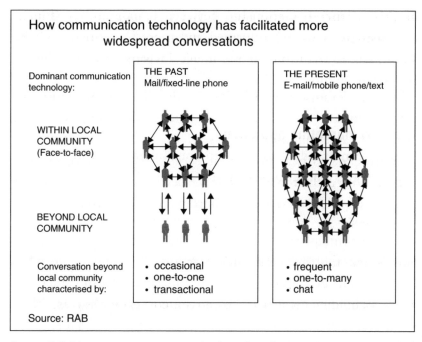

How communication technology has facilitated more widespread conversations

Figure 7.5 How communication technology has facilitated more widespread conversations

they can't be there to converse face to face (Figure 7.5). This has resulted in more widespread conversations amongst more people on a more frequent basis (to illustrate this, just think about how you use e-mail to have lots of small 'conversations' with groups of people that probably wouldn't take place by telephone).

This growth in dialogue has implications for the business world, as highlighted on *The Cluetrain Manifesto* website. The manifesto claims that traditional business isn't working because people are talking more, helped by the Internet (and other technology). The authors present a simple choice to businessmen – understand that markets are conversations, and that customers will have these conversations whether you like it or not, or lose your business.

In this context, it seems logical that word of mouth will be an increasingly powerful communication tool for brands – John Grant has referred to it as 'the new television'.

This was demonstrated in MEC MediaLab's recent report into word of mouth (*Where's Debbie?*), where consumers were asked which of a range of information sources would make them 'more comfortable' with a product or service from a company (see Figure 7.6). At the top of the list was a friend's recommendation, which people deemed more important than even their own past experiences.

So it's clear that word of mouth is important for consumers when they are considering companies – but its power doesn't end there. Once individuals feel trust towards a company, they are likely

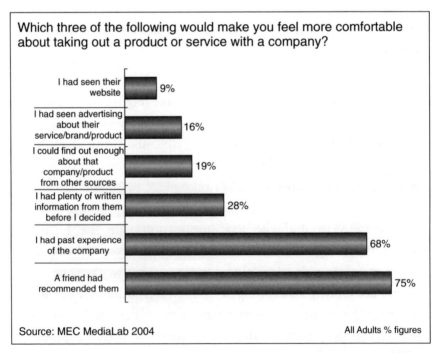

Which three of the following would make you feel more comfortable about taking out a product or service with a company?

I had seen their website — 9%

I had seen advertising about their service/brand/product — 16%

I could find out enough about that company/product from other sources — 19%

I had plenty of written information from them before I decided — 28%

I had past experience of the company — 68%

A friend had recommended them — 75%

Source: MEC MediaLab 2004 — All Adults % figures

Figure 7.6 Factors making consumers 'more comfortable' with a product or service

to become powerful advocates for it themselves, as illustrated in the Henley Centre research in Figure 7.7. The Henley Centre highlights the growth of a 'Referral Economy' in the UK, reflecting the influence of word of mouth on purchasing decisions.

In *After Image*, John Grant asserts that conversation is the best means of building trust between people and brands. And as The Henley Centre research demonstrates, if people trust a brand they are likely to become powerful advocates of that brand.

Having defined the importance of it, how can companies influence and propagate word of mouth? In particular, this seems to present a huge challenge to advertising.

Interestingly, the MEC MediaLab report suggests that transmitters' of word of mouth are more brand-literate and more responsive to communications. Advertising is identified as having the potential to be as powerful in driving word of mouth as any other element of the brand mix, providing it speaks with people in an appropriate way.

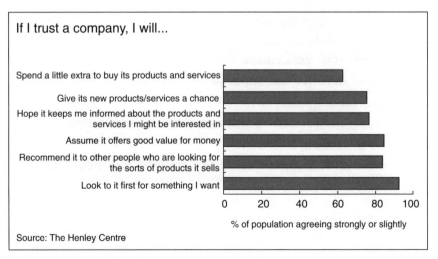

Figure 7.7 Once individuals feel trust towards a company, other benefits

The report highlights the idea of creating conversations with 'transmitters' to help them engage with and understand brand ideas.

7.4 Summary

- Growing consumer cynicism in institutions and brands means that brands have to continually earn the trust of their customers.
- As people have become more aware of their value to companies, they have become more empowered in their role as consumers.
- The increasing accessibility of information is helping to educate people about companies and inform their decision-making.
- Consumers are making more active choices about brands based on real information.
- The influence of image advertising in many markets is being reduced.
- In this evolving context, brands need to be more approachable, involving, and participative to encourage consumers to engage with them.
- A global resurgence in dialogue is taking place.
- Word of mouth is an important driver for people in considering a brand or company.
- Word of mouth can be influenced by managed communications (including advertising).
- Involving consumers in conversations can help develop greater trust in a brand.

8
Radio's Role in Emerging Brand Thinking

If 'dialogue' between brand and consumer promises to be one of the strongest components of marketing in the future, where does that leave radio – a medium which we have seen is essentially conversational in nature?

If radio's version of 'brand dialogue' is the more informal 'brand conversation', what is the role and importance of this?

This chapter examines the concept of brand conversation, and how it can work for brands, in detail.

8.1 Radio as a brand conversation medium

In the previous chapter we reviewed how societal trends are changing consumer behaviour towards brands, and how this is leading brands towards a more 'conversational' form of marketing.

So how well can individual media help to meet this challenge? In this section we explore the key traits of radio that help define it as a conversation medium.

Radio has a spontaneous feel

Radio editorial is characterised by strands of live programming. Compare this with TV, which mainly consists of a series of pre-recorded individual programmes, or the press, where any article was written at the latest the day before, and you begin to understand why radio listeners feel that the medium is more spontaneous and flexible.

Whilst presenters have less flexibility these days in terms of the music they play, and the overall structure of a show tends to be decided in advance, the detail of what presenters say and how they say it is driven by the context of the moment. Many different factors, e.g. a phone call/e-mail/text from a listener, comments from, or a conversation with, a co-presenter or the weather/traffic report, can influence the spontaneity of the moment.

Listeners recognise this greater level of spontaneity on radio in terms of how lively the medium feels (see Figure 8.1). In fact, radio is the only broadcast medium where the consumer regularly has an immediate catalytic effect on editorial content.

'Hearing a beloved song on the radio is as near as godless teens get to a religious experience . . . pop radio has brought home to

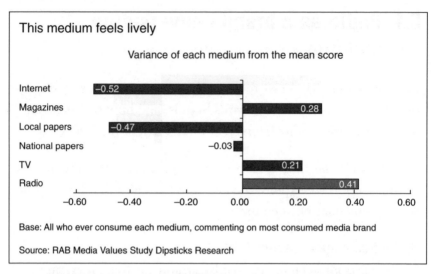

Figure 8.1 Comparison of different media in terms of feeling lively

people the transcendent purity of hearing a favourite song at random.'

Julie Burchill

Another indicator of radio's spontaneity is how highly people score the medium compared with others in relation to its ability to propagate gossip (see Figure 8.2).

The live nature of programming and its ability to flex to meet the demands of the latest news and gossip make radio a valuable medium for brands that are keen to generate a more spontaneous/instantaneous response from the listener.

Radio operates on a human/personal level

We have already revealed that the majority of people listen to radio on their own. What does this mean for the way radio communicates?

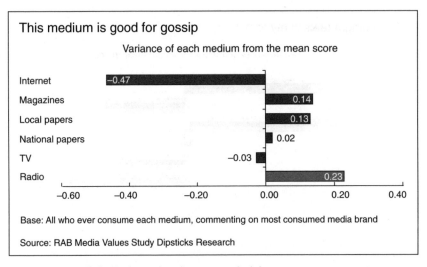

Figure 8.2 Each medium's perceived ability to propagate gossip

Even if people are listening when other people are around, radio is still very rarely a group experience: they will have their own personal experience of the output that is not shared with other people. Their inner eye and their feelings are doing the work.

This is a stark contrast to cinema, for example, where there is a strong sense of audience – and the cinema audience often reacts as a united crowd, for example if ads come over as patronising or silly.

Radio presenters actively cultivate the apparent illusion of intimacy with radio – it is a core part of presenters' training that they must learn to speak to an individual rather than an audience. The success of this approach is reflected in the research detailed in Figure 8.3 demonstrating that people are more likely to feel that radio speaks at their level than any other medium.

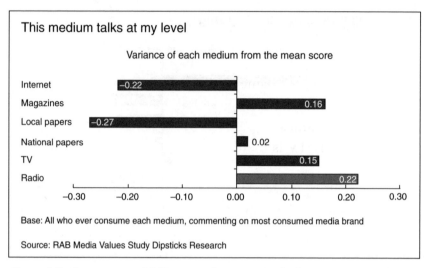

Figure 8.3 Comparison of different media in terms of talking at consumer's level

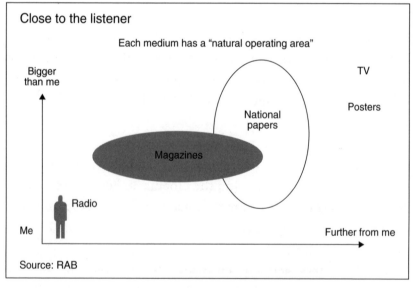

Figure 8.4 Each medium has a 'natural operating area'

So, despite the fact that radio is a broadcast medium, its intimacy offers the advertiser the chance to speak to the listener on a one-to-one basis that in turn creates a sense of being 'on my level' and 'closer to me' than other media (see Figure 8.4).

Radio conversations are ongoing

In the section reviewing how and why people listen, the habitual nature of radio listening was explored. Even lighter listeners tune into radio at the same time, every day – especially during the working week. In fact, according to research (RAB *Media Values Study*), almost three-quarters of radio listeners tune in every day – only TV is more regularly consumed (Figure 8.5).

It is not really surprising to discover that the media people consume most regularly are also the ones that score most highly in terms of helping them feel connected to the outside world (Figure 8.6). However, it is interesting to note that radio outscores TV in this respect, despite having a lower proportion of daily listeners within its overall audience. This is likely to stem from radio being used more as a solitude management medium, as highlighted earlier.

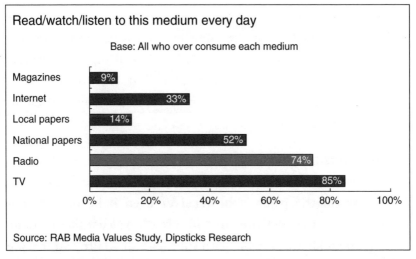

Figure 8.5 Percentage of people consuming each medium on a daily basis

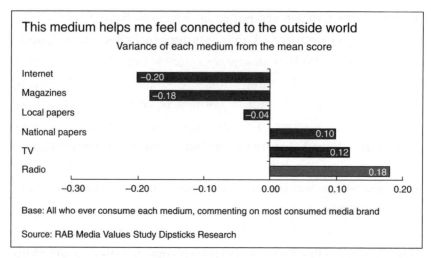

Figure 8.6 Comparison of different media in terms of making an individual feel connected to the outside world

So radio is used every day by people to help connect them to the outside world when they are on their own – heavier listeners may tune in for hours at a time, especially if radio is an accompaniment to their working day.

The overall effect of this is that the listener has a greater sense of being involved in an ongoing conversation with the presenters, which is revisited on a daily basis. It also presents an opportunity for brands to involve listeners in their own ongoing and regularly updated conversation by exploiting relevant habitual listening patterns.

Radio invites response

All communications are two-way, in the sense that they create a reaction on the part of the receiver even if he/she has not physically responded. Compared to other broadcast media, radio is very much about two-way communication – both in terms of mental and physical response.

In terms of mental response, radio listeners have a subtle type of involvement with their radio station. In *Radio Days 2*, 43 % of listeners agreed that:

'I find myself talking back to the people on the radio.'

Mostly this talking is private, or even mental, and goes unheard. More recent research backs up this statistic by demonstrating how consumers feel they talk back to radio more than any other medium (Figure 8.7).

But equally, radio draws plenty of physical participation from the listeners – phone-ins, dedications, competitions, promotions, helplines, etc. (participation levels are shown in Figure 8.8).

The reasons for this high level of physical involvement and interactivity are complex. At a basic level, it is about the cultural norms of radio – rarely an hour goes by without the presenter

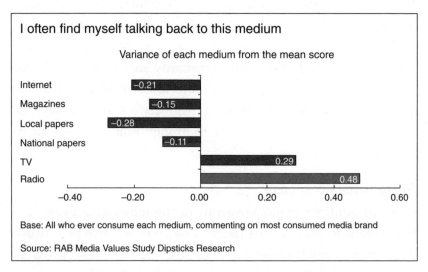

Figure 8.7 Comparison of how many people claim to 'talk back' to different media

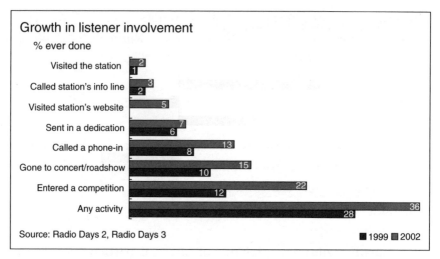

Figure 8.8 Growth in listener involvement with radio stations

inviting the listener to phone/text/e-mail their thoughts on a particular topic of conversation, or to enter a competition.

Another reason is the relationship of trust between station and listener – listeners feel the station is a benign power, and they won't be humiliated or ripped off, so getting involved is low-risk.

A further reason is that radio is primarily about music and talk, both of which are very personal, emotional areas – we have an instinctive reaction to music (positively or otherwise) and we instinctively tend to react to things that are said to us personally.

Radio is tonal

Commercial radio is predominantly a combination of music and the spoken word, and this means that tone of voice or attitude come over strongly. Research demonstrates that radio's tone of voice reflects that of its listeners – people feel that radio is the medium that most 'speaks their language' (Figure 8.9).

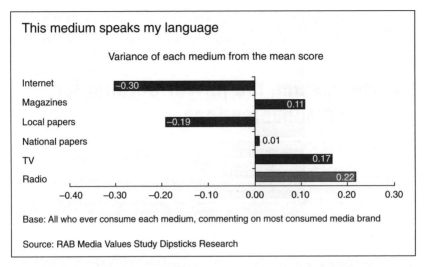

Figure 8.9 Comparison of different media in terms of speaking the consumer's language

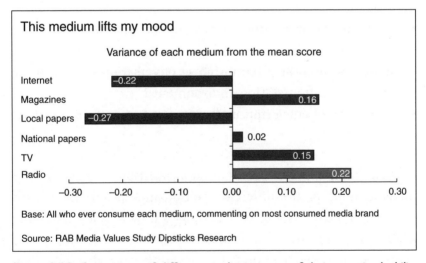

Figure 8.10 Comparison of different media in terms of their perceived ability to lift the consumer's mood

Radio's tonal qualities mean that it is a powerful medium for affecting people's mood/influencing how they feel. Research highlights that radio has a positive, uplifting tone – consumers classify it as the best medium for 'lifting my mood' (Figure 8.10).

The tonal strengths of radio are valuable for advertisers who are keen to positively influence how listeners feel about their brand.

8.2 Harnessing the power of radio for brand conversations

In this section we explore how radio's conversational qualities open up a new set of possibilities for brands communicating with radio listeners, both in terms of media planning and creative content.

From a media perspective, brand conversation invites questions about the context within which a brand should converse with its customers in order to establish the most effective connection.

- When is the best time to have a conversation with your customers?
- Where is the best place for this conversation to take place (listener location/station environment)?
- What type of conversation do you want to have (rational vs. emotional)?

To help answer these questions, it is valuable to have greater understanding of the different relationships people have with their radio. Below is a brief overview of how people's listen-ing needs vary (for more information on how listening varies across the day, see Section 2.1). Newslink have also published research into listener modes and mindsets (available at www. capitalradiogroup.com/commercial/newslink) that can also help inform planning in this context.

Functional vs. emotional listening

There are two key facets to listeners' requirements from radio – the first is a functional requirement, while the second is an emotional one.

The functional requirement is the need for information – news, time checks, traffic news, weather or sports results. In previous RAB research, one respondent described how listening to the radio could make the difference between her journey to work taking 30 minutes or an hour and a half.

The emotional requirement is characterised by listeners in terms of the relationship they have with either a presenter or a particular music show.

The reality of people's daily patterns is that the two requirements are not mutually exclusive – the balance between them changes across the course of a day according to listeners' moods, with stations being chosen according to the mood of the moment.

Habitual and discretionary listening

There are two broad types of listening – habitual and discretionary. They aren't mutually exclusive as there is an element of discretion in habitual listening and an element of habit in discretionary listening.

It is broadly the case that habitual listening occurs at times of peak radio listening, getting ready for work and in the office itself. Discretionary listening takes place at times of greater leisure (e.g. in the evening) and involves greater commitment on the part of the listener.

Listeners tend to wake up to their station of 'habitual' listening, and then cherry-pick programmes from their repertoire of programmes/stations across the day.

Considerations for developing brand conversations on radio

Having understood how listening varies in character depending upon time of day/habitual vs. discretional/station environment, what are the contextual factors that should be considered for developing optimum brand conversations on radio?

- *Type of product being advertised*. Some product sectors may be associated more with rational or emotional conversations. Note that certain brands within a sector may go against the grain.
- *Type of marketing message*. It might be more appropriate for brands to speak more intensely (or have a more relaxed conversation) when listening is more discretionary. More pithy, transactional conversations could be more relevant during periods of functional listening.
- *Type of environment*. Consideration needs to be given to whether a particular radio station, programme or presenter holds more appeal from a rational or emotional perspective. Sponsorship and promotions may be particularly effective in taking advantage of these different types of conversational context.
- *Listener location/activity*. Certain brand conversation may relate to particular listener locations (e.g. in-car) or activities (e.g. housework).

8.3 New conversational roles for radio

In this section we explore the potential new roles that radio can play for brands within the context of brand conversation.

The following ideas for creating brand conversations using radio were presented by John Grant at the Media Planners' Forum, held at the IPA on the 30th September 2003.

Advertisers that have already explored some of this territory have been highlighted under the relevant categories. Many of these examples can be found on www.better-radio-advertising.co.uk.

Conversation about vision and values
Radio is a powerfully emotive medium (Marshall McLuhan claimed it 'caused' Hitler and Churchill). As a result, it offers a good opportunity to talk about brand values from a human perspective.

> *Example:* Carphone Warehouse and Egg have both used real staff to talk about their company's values in a meaningful way for their customers.

Conversation between media
Radio adds something that the Internet can't do for itself: *outreach* (TV and cinema are too expensive and remote from net usage). So radio is a great way of reaching out to people and getting them to engage with new websites.

> *Example:* Confetti.co.uk used the fact that radio is often used to accompany Internet sessions to persuade people already online to visit their website. They were able to spot when radio ads had been broadcast from the increase in hits on their website.

Conversation between confidants
Radio has a 'whisper in my ear'/gossip appeal that can give the impression that the listener is eavesdropping on a personal conversation.

> *Example:* Nestlé Double Crème ran a radio promotion where people had to phone up their loved ones and persuade them to 'bunk-off' work to meet them at home for a love tryst.

Conversation that's really catchy

Radio has a 'word in your shell-like' factor and can be helpful in spreading particular types of information by word of mouth.

> *Example:* IKEA ran an outrageous announcement banning people wearing beards from using their Bristol store.

Conversation between individuals

Radio production costs mean that individualised communication is relatively affordable and accessible, compared with other media. This allows brands the opportunity to broadcast personal messages from/to their individual brand users.

Conversation of consensus

Radio is an authentic medium where the voice can carry authority, warmth and experience. Brands could be part of a conversation that helps educate people about specific issues and/or new areas of interest, through the experience of people already in that field.

> *Example:* On behalf of the Inland Revenue, COI Communications ran ads for Family Tax Credits to help people understand if and how they might qualify for new tax benefits by highlighting how different changes in circumstances can trigger these benefits.

Conversation that helps people grow

Radio (the voice) is more cultured and enabling than 'image' media. These hidden strengths can be exploited by brands to help individuals develop themselves.

Example: American Express ran a celebrity-based interview show focusing on interviews with people who have fulfilled their dreams to highlight how AMEX could contribute to the achievement and facilitation of ambitions.

Conversation that restores subjectivity

TV and magazines flatten the world with global stereotypes, clichés and formats. Radio takes broadcasting down to the most local level, allowing brands to speak to people in local accents about local issues.

Example: BT ran ads with different regional accents on different stations to reinforce their relevance to individual communities.

Conversation as bulletin

Radio has an immediacy and newsworthiness that can drive immediate consumer response (e.g. 'go now to this store and get this discount').

Example: Jaffa Cakes built on their role as the favoured biscuit of the England national team by running different ads relating to the previous day's matches every morning across the duration of the 2002 Football World Cup.

8.4 Summary

- Research underpins the differences between the media values of radio and those of other mainstream media, and reinforces the main conversational aspects of the medium (e.g. people are more likely to 'talk back' to radio than any other medium).
- There are five main characteristics of radio that define the medium's conversational qualities:
  — spontaneity;
  — human/personal;
  — ongoing;
  — invites response;
  — tonal.
- These characteristics mean that radio is a particularly useful medium for brands that want to communicate with people in a more conversational manner.
- People's reasons for tuning into the radio differ by time of day and day of week, revolving around two key elements – the functional and the emotional.
- Deeper analysis of listeners' use of radio also reveals that there are two types of radio listening – habitual and discretionary.
- These differing contexts allow brands to develop more engaging conversations by speaking with customers in the most relevant frame of mind.
- Some companies have already explored some of the territory opened up by the brand conversation theme, providing some interesting pointers on the potential applications for other brands.

SECTION 4
THE SEVEN-STEP GUIDE TO BETTER RADIO ADVERTISING

If you want advanced level advertising, what can you as the advertiser actually *do*?

This is the bit where we summarise the seven main steps that advertisers can take to gain more control of the creative development process for radio and achieve a higher, and more effective, level of creativity.

Use this chapter as an aide-mémoire – for daily radio advertising decisions, this is where to stick the bookmark.

Chapter 9 The Seven-Step Guide to Better Radio Advertising

- Step 1: Define a clear role for radio
- Step 2: Keep the brief simple
- Step 3: Ask for the team with radio skills
- Step 4: Take care over tone
- Step 5: Use the right judging criteria
- Step 6: Use preproduction
- Step 7: Consider using a director
- Summary

9
The Seven-Step Guide to Better Radio Advertising

Step 1: Define a clear role for radio
Step 2: Keep the brief simple
Step 3: Ask for the team with radio skills
Step 4: Take care over tone
Step 5: Use the right judging criteria
Step 6: Use preproduction
Step 7: Consider using a director
Summary

The seven-step guide is adapted from a presentation entitled How to be a good client for radio *made by Ralph van Dijk (of Eardrum) and Adrian Reith (of Radioville) at the 2004 RAB Advertiser Conference,* Getting serious with radio creativity.

Their hypothesis was that if advertisers took a more active and positive role within the process and accepted greater responsibility for the outcome, then their radio advertising would be significantly enhanced. They recommended a series of steps that responsible advertisers should take to help them achieve advanced level radio.

We have summarised and adapted the steps they presented to act as a useful reminder to readers of some of the key themes explored in this book.

Step 1: Define a clear role for radio

'Ideas that wouldn't work on radio. A half-hour special entitled "How to tie knots".'

suggested in Crisell, *Understanding Radio*

'The unique strength of radio lies in its power to stir the imagination.'

Roman and Maas, *How to Advertise*

The start point in the creative development process is to have a clear understanding of the role radio is playing within the communications mix, as this should be the primary influence upon the creative brief.

Radio is a highly flexible medium, which means it is often asked to perform challenging tasks. It *can* carry detailed information, it *can* be booked relatively late, and it *can* be produced at short notice and at low cost, but these tend to work against high quality creativity. Advertisers have to take account of this and realise there are compromises to be made.

Functional roles might include maintaining communication between bursts of other media; reaching people at relevant times; encouraging people to respond to other media (e.g. Internet); and communicating a variety of messages.

The functional role of radio will have a direct impact on what information is necessary to include in the brief. For example, if the role of radio is to stimulate the listener to seek out and respond to another medium, it may not require all of the product detail.

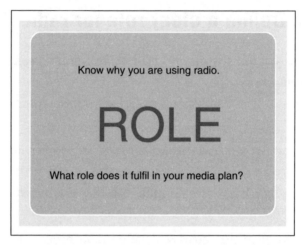

Emotional roles might include getting closer to consumers; becoming part of their daily lives; speaking with them at a more human level; and giving a brand a voice.

In reality, because it relies on the spoken word, all radio advertising influences the emotional feelings of the listener towards the brand, whether this is intended or not. So it makes sense to consider what emotional effect you'd like your radio advertising to have, even if this is just to reinforce current brand perceptions.

Step 2: Keep the brief simple

'Say it simply, say it dramatically, and be completely single-minded about your claim.'
                    Alastair Crompton, *The Craft of Copywriting*

Probably the most commonly proffered advice for anyone planning advertising communication, 'keep it simple' helps the brief stay focused and ensures that the creative team can concentrate on dramatising a single proposition effectively, rather than reeling off a list of brand benefits. This advice is often illustrated with the 'catch one ball' vs. 'drop all three balls' analogy.

Despite an almost universal understanding of why simplicity is important in advertising, it seems that the rulebook is thrown out of the window when it comes to radio. On occasions it appears that dedication to the task of keeping the TV and poster work simple and focused often leads advertisers to shoehorn all of the detail into their radio briefs. This spells disaster on two fronts:

1. Complex information written on the page is a lot easier for the brain to process than complex information given verbally. As a simple illustration of this, have a look at the script for AMD Athlon (Appendix 2) then listen to the ad on www. better-radio-advertising.co.uk *without looking at the script.*

   How much detail did you really manage to take out of the radio commercial?

2. A brief packed with information leaves little room for the creative to engage the listener subconsciously on an emotional level. This will result in the listener 'zoning out' and (unless it features a recognisable sonic branding property) will reduce the effectiveness of the commercial.

Create room for emotional connection in the brief.

SIMPLICITY

One message per commercial

Remember the golden rule: One message per commercial . . . if you have more messages, make more commercials. After all, with radio you can afford to!

Step 3: Ask for the team with radio skills

'With TV, the palette is huge, with an endless range of colours and brushes available. With radio, you only have a pencil – so how you use that pencil – technique – becomes paramount.'

Brian Jenkins, COI Communications

'Despite the trend to a more integrated approach, many main-stream advertising agencies could be called "TV agencies" because that is where their creative interests lie – most people in agencies still love making little films more than anything else.'

John Grant, author of *After Image*

These two quotes sum up one of the biggest challenges facing creativity in radio advertising. It is a medium that requires a high level of craft skills yet the companies that are most commonly tasked with writing for the medium are more passionate about visual media.

However, this is at a company level. Within almost every main-stream advertising agency creative department there are two or three creative teams that enjoy writing for radio. And because they enjoy writing for radio, they tend to be given more radio briefs to work on. As a result, they are more motivated by radio briefs and, most importantly, are more skilled in writing for the medium.

So, if you're briefing radio, ask for the creative team with radio skills to work on it. If the writers are radio-friendly, they're more likely to help out with potential fault lines in the brief and have a better understanding of how to find the most effective compromise between getting your message across and irritating the listener.

Step 4: Take care over tone

'Listening to a message is much more effective than reading it ... the tone of the human voice gives the words emotional impact that the printed words can never achieve.'
Jack Trout and Al Ries, *Which is more powerful, the eye or the ear?*

If you didn't know it before reading this book, you should by now be fully aware of the strength of radio advertising in affecting the listener's feelings about a brand. This effect applies no matter whether the reason for advertising is tactical or strategic, product or brand-focused.

The result of this is that you must clarify in the brief the kind of impression you want your brand to leave. Think about how you want to come across and express this clearly. Play to radio's strengths – use words that describe how people relate to each other, rather than bland corporate statements (all brands seem to want to be seen as authoritative, contemporary and innovative).

For examples of how tone can vary dramatically, have a listen to the *Land of Leather* and *Waitrose* commercials on www.better-radio-advertising.co.uk. Both are retailers promoting their latest offers, yet their tone is completely different – *Land of Leather* comes across as a market trader, whilst *Waitrose* speaks with the tone of a sophisticated acquaintance.

Tone is an important part of the brief but how this eventually translates to the listener is all in the execution – more on this subject in Step 5.

Above all, when considering your tone of voice, remember to respect the listener.

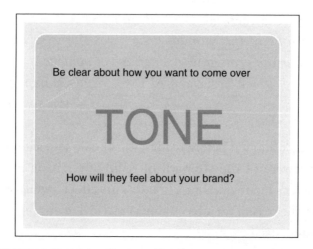

Step 5: Use the right judging criteria

'If a feature film can't please everybody, if a novel can't please everybody, if music by a great composer can't please everybody, how can one ad please everybody?'
Alastair Crompton, *The Craft of Copywriting*

Judging is a challenging stage of the process for advertising in any medium, but perhaps even more so with radio because it is the only medium where there are no visuals to help.

This leads to a terrible temptation to look at the *words*. And this can be fatal when judging radio. The words are concrete, whereas the emotions that engage the listener (and influence how they feel about your brand) live in the gaps *between* the words.

So, how can you judge what is *not* written? Ask for the script to be brought to life by being read out or even recorded (but note – demo versions aren't always helpful). Storyboards can also be helpful, as can the use of audio material from elsewhere to explain the intended tone of the ads.

Having done this, you may feel confident that the commercial will engage the listener emotionally but will your brand benefit from this in the intended way? The three key questions that we recommend for judging radio ideas are:

1. What will make the listener zone in?
2. How is this linked to the brand and its message?
3. What tonal impression of the brand will the advertising leave with the listener?

Consider using these techniques when selling radio work on within your own company – they are valuable for protecting the good ideas.

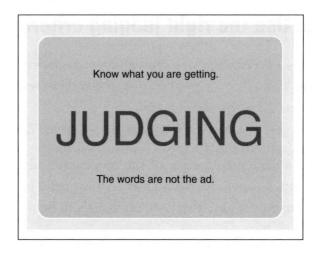

Step 6: Use preproduction

'Look at how much time we spend over a voice-over on television, then when it comes to radio we sort of go – oh yes, so-and-so, he'll do, right, off you go. Where in fact it's ten times more important.'

John Hegarty

Radio advertising in the production stage of the creative development process is just as fragile as it is in the briefing and judging stages, and requires similar attention to relevant detail. As we covered in Section 2.3, listeners are very sensitive to the way things come over on the radio, so mistakes made during production have the capacity to completely undermine a strong radio idea and ultimately limit its effectiveness.

And that is why it is important to agree things in preproduction (don't wait for your agency to organise this – it's not common practice for creative agencies to run preprods for radio, so it may never happen!). Preproduction enables all of the stakeholders in the radio campaign to head off any potential problems before they get to the studio. This will save time (and money) in the studio and ensure that everyone is concentrating on getting the best performance rather than resolving unrelated issues.

As a guide, here are some of the issues that should be agreed at the preproduction stage:

- Is the script really 30 seconds?
- How much legal copy is required, if any? What effect will this have on the overall time-length?
- What music is going to be used and are there usage issues?
- Are sound effects required? Does the studio have these and will they do the job required of them?
- Who are we casting? Why are they the most suitable person for this role?

Finally, it is worth noting that commercials can develop greatly during production – actors and directors can find better ways to bring the scenes to life, funnier ways of making the dialogue work, etc. It is important to agree in advance whether you are

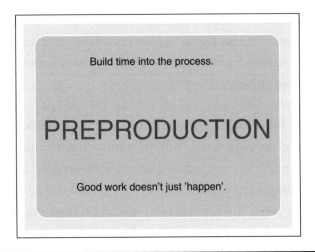

Build time into the process.

PREPRODUCTION

Good work doesn't just 'happen'.

prepared to leave room for this in the process and how much freedom you are prepared to offer.

Step 7: Consider using a director

'I have no idea what to do in a radio studio. We have seen half a dozen of our scripts made, and sometimes they work out well, sometimes they're terrible.'

Anonymous agency creative

A lot of radio's power lies in the subtext – not *what* is said, but *how* it is said. It is a common misconception that hiring a good voice artist will ensure a good performance, no matter what. But as with film and TV, this simply isn't true – the artist in the studio does not magically share the vision of the writers. So to get the best radio ads you need to enlist the help of someone who is experienced in getting the most out of a script – a director. And the more adventurous the idea, the more direction the artist will need.

Yet radio is the one medium where creatives get to direct the actors themselves. In one way this is great, because it allows the creatives to define exactly how the commercial is going to turn out. But in another way it is very scary – few creatives have had any training in directing actors, and some actors are much harder to direct than others.

You may be lucky and have a writer who is experienced in directing working on your brief, but in reality the chances are you won't, so speak to your agency about investing in a specialist radio director (in the same way that you would use a professional TV director for a TV commercial and a professional photographer or illustrator for your print work).

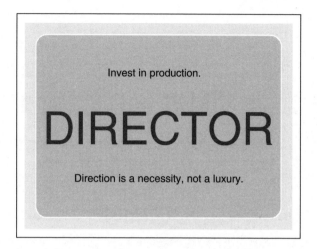

Invest in production.

DIRECTOR

Direction is a necessity, not a luxury.

The additional cost of hiring a radio director is not prohibitive and, in relation to the media investment behind your commercial(s), is insignificant. An additional benefit of hiring a director is that they will normally manage the preproduction stage for you.

Summary

- Advertisers can make a huge difference to the quality of their radio advertising by taking more responsibility for its development across the whole process.
- The seven steps to advanced level radio advertising provide a simple guide to the crucial parts of the process that advertisers can, and should, exert an influence over.
- The guide demonstrates how better radio creativity can be achieved in a harmonious manner by augmenting the efforts of everybody involved in the process.

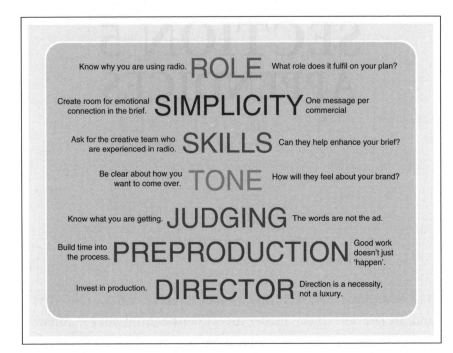

As a final thought, it should be noted that the seven steps aren't about instantly achieving 'great' radio advertising, but about helping to 'raise the bar'. If this doesn't happen immediately, they will at least provide a framework for understanding why this didn't happen and how to improve things next time around.

SECTION 5
APPENDICES

Appendix 1
The RAB Bus Research Study

The Bus Research methodology was devised to create an effective 'distracted listening' environment for testing response to radio commercials. Under normal conditions, response is either difficult to gauge (it's difficult to find listeners who have certainly been exposed to the campaigns on air) or the method is too intensive to be representative of reality (asking consumers to deliberately sit and listen to ads and then give opinions).

The RAB Research Bus method involved fifty members of the public being invited to take part in a test ostensibly about coach travel, where they sat on a coach during a half-hour journey. During the journey, the radio appeared to be on in the coach: in fact the output was carefully created to sound like their usual radio station, and six ads were played twice each during the journey. The respondents were then taken to a separate building and, having had the real purpose of the test explained to them, asked to complete a questionnaire about their memories of the radio output.

The questionnaire captured spontaneous memories (any output), then brand-name prompted memories, then recall prompted by audio-snippets, and finally, the respondents listened to all the ads again and were asked more detailed questions about recall and communication.

The purpose of the test was to discover whether this methodology worked, and the result showed that it did. Within the detail of the six campaigns, the following findings were also evident:

- although all six ads had exactly the same exposure, recall levels varied very widely;
- ads which were enjoyable and/or clear were recalled much more strongly than ads which were confusing or boring;
- some ads and messages were more strongly recalled than the relevant brands – identifying weak brand linkage.

Appendix 2
Radio Script

Brand: AMD Athlon XP 1800+ Processor
Time length: 30"

FVO: Thanks to AMD's Quanta-Speed technology, operating at 1.533 GHz, a PC with a new AMD Athlon XP 1800+ processor out-performs a PC with a 1.8 GHz Pentium 4 processor on the applications you use most.

There, not going too fast was I?

The new AMD Athlon XP processor – a new kind of fast.

Appendix 3
Online Radio Ads Track Listing

	Brand	Ad	Notes	Workshop delegates say
1	Dove	Lipsticks	A compelling opening, but the link is with 'difficult decisions' rather than the brand and its benefits	'Easy ad to sell, because client likes the end and creatives like the beginning' (account director) 'Starts off well' 'We call that borrowed interest – doesn't work'
2	Opel Corsa	Belgian singalong	A very unusual treatment: almost entirely sung by a choir	'So bad it's good?' 'Why don't other brands do this?'
3	Carphone Warehouse	Pay As You Go	These ads built a brand on radio – very straight announcement on a sound bed.	'If you're not in the market, all you get is the brand and the feel' 'Dull ... but

	Brand	Ad	Notes	Workshop delegates say
			This ad was one of hundreds over the years.	clearly effective' 'Fabulous music property'
4	Apple Tango	Lost Property	Captivating – keeps the listener guessing. As in other media, one single idea taken to the extreme (dubious relationship with a soft drink)	'Absolutely unique' 'A brilliant take on the wind-up phone call'
5	AMD	Athlon 1800+	Very detailed announcement of the product benefits, but hard for normal listeners to comprehend	'Aimed at IT managers?' 'Looks straight-forward enough on paper' 'Gobbledy gook'
6	COI Army recruitment	Anti-tank	The listener is taken on a 'test-drive' for being in the army. Challenging, but in a way that is not daft or self-indulgent.	'Very visual ad' 'Compelling' 'So – which one was it?' 'Would strongly affect brand perceptions'

	Brand	Ad	Notes	Workshop delegates say
7	Nivea for Men	Parking	Neat dramatisation of the joke about men who use cosmetics being 'girly'	'Great double joke' 'The brand resolves the riddle of the ad' 'Humour is relevant and appealing'
8	Hamlet Cigars	Bummer – couple going out	Great use of a dramatic device established over 35 years – the 'Hamlet moment'	'Priceless' 'Beautiful casting, acting and direction' 'A joke yes, but well told, so bears repetition'
9	Tennent's Dry	Epic dryness tableau	Extraordinary scenes depicted about dryness; proof that radio can go anywhere	'I didn't get that it was to do with dryness' 'Weird and interesting but too long, I zoned out'
10	Woolwich	Houston launch	Builds tension but payoff is too complicated	'I would tune out of the second half' 'As soon as the

	Brand	Ad	Notes	Workshop delegates say
				voice-over comes in with a weak link, the listener knows the entertaiment is over'
11	British Airways	Sonic	Extract from Delibes' *Lakme* which has become a powerful BA branding device	'What a find that music was' 'They use it everywhere' 'Instant brand values: just add words!'
12	British Airways	Sitar and Piano	Great exploitation of the BA music: evocative and very poised	'Captivating' 'You expect them to start waffling on about special offers, like most ads do – but they don't. It's great' 'Pure brand – no tactical content'
13	Hang Up The Phone	Sound Art (not a commercial, but written for a commercial	Makes the point that weird or unusual sounds cannot alone captivate the	'Boring!' 'Starts off kind of interesting, but then ... who cares'

Brand	Ad	Notes	Workshop delegates say
	which never ran)	attention of the listener	'Self indulgent' 'Not surprised it never ran'
14 Barclays Bank	Violin	Uses an irritating noise to ensure the listener's attention	'Horrible: I feel picked on' 'They think you will sympathise with the voice-over's apparent irritation – but it's the overall ad that's irritating'
15 Mace	Leap Year Low prices	A popular form of radio ad in the 80s and 90s – a leaflet disguised as a telephone conversation	'Can't remember a single product' 'Patronising' 'Gives the oppo-site of the effect they want'
16 Eagle Star	Daddy's broken down	Nicely drawn scene – a story entertainingly told, with winning performance from the child actor	'Funny and relevant' 'Appeals to parents'

	Brand	Ad	Notes	Workshop delegates say
17	Beamish Stout	Wind	Donald Sutherland using his story-telling skills to create an atmosphere for the brand	'Actually poetic' 'Stout market has moved on now, but this was so distinctive at the time'
18	Confetti	Wedding Dress	OTT wacky humour but done with great timing	'Gives a good tonality to the Confetti brand – friendly, fun, sympathetic' 'Brand-level radio'
19	Hamlet Cigars	Potato Head	Great use of a dramatic device established over 35 years – the 'Hamlet moment'	'We've all been there' 'Look what can happen when radio isn't trying to convey endless offers and facts'
20	Wella Shock Waves	Toilet	Cunning product demonstration ad – pacy, strong humour	'It's all about the product' 'Teenage boys would be saying that in the playground'

	Brand	Ad	Notes	Workshop delegates say
21	Carphone Warehouse	Mark Tomlinson	An extension of the music-based campaign which focuses on staff to change perceptions of the stores	'Designed to humanise the brand – which is what it does' 'Won't win any prizes, but it's not supposed to. It's supposed to change people's views'
22	Egg	Mindy Chowhan	Egg focused on how its staff were individuals, offering a service for individuals	'Unexpected, very personal' 'Exploits the natural charm of the staff to make a point' 'Very soft sell. You wouldn't necessarily get it the first time – but you'd hear it again then'
23	Nestlé Double Crème	Promotional airtime, not advertising. Listeners tried to win holidays by tempting	Very funny as we eavesdrop on Lorraine trying to lure home her policeman partner Steve,	'Everyone would be talking about that' 'You want her to win and he's being such a twit'

Brand	Ad	Notes	Workshop delegates say
	their partners home	who is on the beat; shows how compelling reality on radio can be, especially in promotions	
24 IKEA	Bristol store opening – ban on visitors with facial hair	A brilliantly attention getting idea expressed fairly simply – until the end	'Anarchic almost' 'A one-off' 'That got national press coverage'
25 COI Family Tax Credits	Entitlements explained	Simple announcement campaign based on relevance – people who qualify will wish to listen	'They have something to say – they just say it' 'Not very creative'
26 American Express	(Promotional trail for sponsored programme) 'Live your dreams'	Trailer uses excerpts of the celebrity inter-view to give a feel for the sponsored programme, rather than detail	'All about dreams' 'A mood pro-gramme, so the trailer creates a mood'

	Brand	Ad	Notes	Workshop delegates say
27	Jaffa Cakes	Hand of Hod	Three examples to show the approach – during the World Cup football, the team rang Japanese hotels to leave messages about Jaffa Cakes	'Brilliant exploitation of the mood of the moment' 'Demonstrates radio's ability to be red-hot topical' 'Very funny'
28	Jaffa Cakes	Big Brother	See above	See above
29	Jaffa Cakes	We'll be back	See above	See above
30	Waitrose	Hot Stuff (one ad in a whole series with similar structure but each using a different piece of music)	The music, unexplained, sets a kind of question: the voice resolves it on behalf of the supermarket brand and its current offers.	'Unusual, has a bit of poise' 'Feels hugely superior to all the other desperate grocery advertising' 'Speaks volumes about the brand'
31	Land of Leather	Clearance sale	Straight announcement: relies on	'Sounds like someone shouting on a market

Brand	Ad	Notes	Workshop delegates say
		relevance (audience have to be already interested)	stall: maybe that's the kind of brand it is' 'Makes them sound cheap' 'Kind of standard radio advertising'
32 Marie Curie Cancer Care	Angel	Moving reworking of the old religious story	'Shows the power of having the right voice' 'Powerful'
33 COI Department of Transport	Don't drive tired	Neatly written, leaving the listener uncomfortable and then shocked	'I started off thinking it might be trying to be funny' 'Incredibly strong to listen to in a car'
34 Woolworth's	3 for 2 DVD offer	Classic retailer offer, but executed with a bit of fun and empathy	'Tells you what the offer is, and the creative sweetens the pill' 'Focuses on the offer – you can't really recall the ad without recaling the offer'

	Brand	Ad	Notes	Workshop delegates say
35	Prudential	Fifty Something	Poetry is rare in advertising, and this campaign showed how it can powerfully connect a brand	'That brand knows exactly who it's talking to' 'I'd feel better about a brand that spoke like that, than the usual advertising rubbish about pensions, etc.'
36	RSPCA	Injection	A dog is put down – the story told, we discover, by the dog himself	'Forces you to think about the issue' 'A message that's strangely intimate and urgent on radio'

References

Castells, M. (2000) *The Rise of the Network Society*, second edition, Blackwell.

Crisell, A. (1986) *Understanding Radio*, Methuen.

Crompton, A. (1979) *The Craft of Copywriting*, Random House Business Books.

dunnhumby (2003) *Radio, the Sales Multiplier Study*, Radio Advertising Bureau.

Grant, J. (2000) *The New Marketing Manifesto*, Texere Publishing.

Grant, J. (2003) *After Image*, Harper Collins.

Jackson, D.M. (2003) *Sonic Branding*, Palgrave Macmillan.

Jackson, D.M. (2004) Listen carefully, *FT Creative Business*, 28th September.

Millward Brown (2000) *The Radio Multiplier Study*, Radio Advertising Bureau.

Roman, K. and Maas, J. (1992) *How to Advertise*, second edition, Kogan Page.

Shingler, M. and Wieringa, C. (1998) *On Air: Methods and Meanings of Radio*, Oxford University Press.

Wiseman, R. (1995) The Megalab Truth Test, *Nature*, 373, 391.

Index